ANGELS AMONG US

Ron Rhodes

HARVEST HOUSE PUBLISHERS
Eugene, Oregon 97402

ANGELS AMONG US

Copyright © 1994 by Harvest House Publishers
Eugene, Oregon 97402

Library of Congress Cataloging-in-Publication Data

Rhodes, Ron.
    Angels among us / by Ron Rhodes.
        p. cm.
    ISBN 1-56507-271-5
    1. Angels. I. Title.
BT966.2.R46   1994
235'.3—dc20   94-22294
                                                                  CIP

Printed in the United States of America.

    95   96   97   98   99   00   01   —   10   9   8   7   6   5   4

*This book is lovingly dedicated
to my grandmother,*

Annie Belle Carothers

Acknowledgments

A special thanks to my wife Kerri for proofreading each chapter in this book for readability purposes prior to publication. Her assistance and encouragement are much appreciated.

Thanks also to our children David and Kylie—my personal cheering squad. (And thanks, kids, for drawing all those pictures for me on the backs of the pages of the first draft of the book. Great art!)

Steve Miller—as always, I appreciate your fine editorial work. (Steve edited two of my earlier books—*Reasoning from the Scriptures with the Jehovah's Witnesses* and *The Culting of America*.) Well done!

To all my friends at the Christian Research Institute and Harvest House Publishers—it's a pleasure working with you. Blessings to you all!

Contents

From the Voice of Angels

Patmos is a mountainous desert island located on the Aegean Sea, about 60 square miles in size. On this desolate island, people were exiled for crimes committed against Rome. The aged apostle John, as a punishment for sharing the good news of Jesus Christ with everyone he met, was exiled here by Domitian, the emperor of Rome. John was sent here to die of either old age or starvation.

Little did John know what God had in store for him on this tiny, secluded island. Somewhere around A.D. 90—some 60 years after Jesus had risen from the dead and ascended to heaven—John had the most sweeping and panoramic vision ever received by a saint of God John was uniquely privileged to behold Christ in His awesome postresurrection glory.

During this incredible vision, John witnessed an unfathomable number of angels singing a song of worship to the Messiah, Jesus Christ:

> I looked and heard the voice of many angels, numbering thousands upon thousands, and ten thousand times ten thousand. They encircled the throne and the living creatures and the elders. In a loud voice they sang: "Worthy is the Lamb, who was slain, to receive power and wealth and wisdom and strength and honor and glory and praise!" (Revelation 5:11-12).

"Ten thousand times ten thousand" is a lot of angels. In fact, this calculates to 100,000,000 (100 million) angels surrounding Christ on the throne, singing a magnificent worship song in praise of Him.

To give you a perspective regarding how many angels this is, the average football stadium in America holds about 50,000 people. It would take some 2,000 stadiums of that size to hold 100,000,000 people. Such large numbers boggle the mind!

Actually, the total number of angels John saw may far exceed 100,000,000. I say this because "ten thousand" was the highest numerical figure used in the Greek language.[1] Hence, "ten thousand times ten thousand" may be John's way of describing an inexpressibly large company of angels—*myriads upon myriads*.

Try to imagine the scene. This magnificent company of at least 100,000,000 angels—with every single one radiating resplendent, luminous beauty—is pictured surrounding Christ's glorious throne and singing praises to His matchless name. The sound of this many voices singing in unison to Christ must surely have been the most awe-inspiring experience John (or any other human) ever encountered. What a precious privilege God bestowed upon His lowly servant!

Note also that in this majestic worship scene, *power*, *glory*, and *honor* are ascribed to Jesus Christ (Revelation 5:12). These are the exact words used to describe the worship of the Father in Revelation 4:11. *Jesus receives from this vast company of angels the same worship as the Father!*

Why do I begin a book on angels in this way? Simply because I want to set the tone for the rest of the book. You see, today there are numerous books being published that focus on angels as an end in themselves, completely (or largely) apart from God. This is not as it should be.

Angels exist because *Christ created them* to exist (Colossians 1:16). Angels exist as eternal servants to God and Christ (Psalm 103:20). Any discussion of angels that treats them as an end in themselves is therefore not balanced.

In chapter 1 we will consider some testimonies of people who claim to have had a close encounter of the *celestial* kind—that is, an encounter with an angel. Then, in chapters 2 and 3, we'll focus our attention on some of the imbalances that have emerged in recent years regarding angels. And throughout the rest of the book we will zero in on what the Bible tells us about this intriguing subject.

As you discover what Scripture has to say, I am confident that you will begin to grasp the glorious provisions God has made for our care and well-being in the world. You will see that angels are indeed among us.

ANGELS
AMONG US

PART 1

Close Encounters of the Celestial Kind

. . . .

*Millions of spiritual creatures
walk the earth unseen, both when we
wake, and when we sleep:
All these with ceaseless praise
his works behold both day and night.*

—John Milton[1]

·1·

Angels in the World Today

Sally, a woman who attends my church, could not restrain her tears as she poured out her heart to Pastor Dave. After a series of medical tests, Sally's doctor had called to inform her that the baby she was expecting would be born with Down's syndrome. Pastor Dave shared Sally's grief at the news. He vowed to help Sally and her husband, Jim, in any way he could.[2]

The following day Pastor Dave decided to send Sally and Jim a postcard with a word of encouragement. On the card, Dave assured them of how much God loved them and their soon-to-be-born little baby.

The postcard ended up being delivered to a wrong address several miles from Sally and Jim's house. Sue—who lived at the house the card was mistakenly delivered to—decided to take the postcard to Sally personally.

When Sally opened the door, Sue said, "This card from your pastor was delivered to my house by mistake. I wanted to come by and deliver the card personally because I, too, have a child with Down's syndrome and I want to help you through this if you'll let me. God has shown me so much that I would like to share with you."

Did the God of all comfort send one of His angels to "reroute" the mail to Sue's house? We can't know for sure, but it seems a good possibility. While the world would tell us that this was just a freak accident, I see the supernatural at work here.

Angels are real. Angels are alive. And, though we rarely perceive it, angels are very much with us here on planet earth.

Christians have always believed in angels. It is not difficult to understand why. After all, the same Bible that attests to the reality and activity of God among His people likewise attests—with *equal vigor*—to the reality and activity of angels in our world. The testimony of Scripture is that there are *innumerable* angels, all active in some capacity in carrying out the bidding of God.

In recent years many believers have spoken of actual encounters with angels. And many of these reports come from quite reliable sources, having the ring of authenticity. As you read the following accounts, I think you will begin to see why I have entitled this book *Angels Among Us*.

Escort into Glory

Evangelist Billy Graham reports that when his maternal grandmother died, the room seemed to fill with a heavenly light. "She sat up in bed and almost laughingly said, 'I see Jesus. He has His arms out-stretched toward me. I see Ben [her husband who had died some years earlier] and I see the angels.' She slumped over, absent from the body but present with the Lord."[3]

Revival in a Hospital

The editor of *Leadership* magazine, a popular publication among church leaders, speaks of how his young daughter was comatose one night, very near death. As reported in *Christianity Today* magazine, a hospital staff worker stopped by the room and witnessed an astonishing sight—angels were hovering over the girl's bed.

By the following morning, the daughter had amazingly revived. This editor—not prone to sensationalism—does not hesitate to believe that angels had truly visited his girl that night.[4] The staff worker—as a result of the incredible sight she had seen—renewed her commitment to God.

Rescue on the Missionary Field

Reverend John G. Paton was a missionary in the New Hebrides Islands.[5] According to his testimony, his mission headquarters was surrounded by hostile natives one night. They apparently intended to burn the building to the ground and put John and his wife to death.

The Patons turned to God. They threw themselves on His mercy. They asked Him to deliver them. They prayed throughout the night. And when the first rays of sunlight came the next morning, the Patons were utterly amazed to see that the natives had left.

About a year later, the chief of that tribe became a Christian. And when Paton asked the chief why the tribe had refrained from burning down the headquarters on that fateful night, the chief surprised him by inquiring, "Who were all those men you had there with you?" Paton answered, "There were no men there—just my wife and I."

The chief then told Paton that he and his warriors had seen hundreds of men standing guard outside the headquarters that night—all dressed in shining garments with swords drawn. These guards completely encircled the headquarters, and the tribe dared not attack.

It was then that Paton realized that God had dispatched His angels to guard him and his wife. As Psalm 34:7 tells us, "the angel of the LORD encamps around those who fear him, and he delivers them." Moreover, "He will command his angels concerning you to guard you in all your ways" (Psalm 91:11).

Paton's testimony sounds remarkably similar to the story of Elisha in 2 Kings 6:15-17. In this story, Elisha and his servant were surrounded by hostile forces. But they were not alone:

> When the servant of the man of God got up and went out early the next morning, an army with horses and chariots had surrounded the city. "Oh, my lord, what shall we do?" the servant asked. "Don't be afraid," the prophet answered. "Those who are with us are more than those who are with them." And Elisha prayed, "O LORD, open his eyes so that he may see." Then the LORD opened the servant's eyes, and he looked and saw the hills full of horses and chariots of fire all around Elisha.

Protection for Children in the Congo

Corrie ten Boom tells of an event that occurred during the Jeunesse Rebellion in the Congo.[6] Some rebels had advanced on a school where about 200 missionary children lived. "They planned to kill both children and teachers," she said. "In the school, they knew of the danger and therefore went to prayer. Their

. . . . .

only protection was a fence and a couple of soldiers, while the enemy, who came closer and closer, amounted to several hundred."

Incredibly, as soon as the rebels came close by, they suddenly turned around and jolted away! The exact same thing happened the next day *and the day after that* when the rebels tried to approach the school.

As providence had it, one of the rebels was wounded and was brought to the missionary hospital. As the doctor was dressing his wounds, he asked the rebel, "Why did you not break into the school as you planned?"

The rebel responded, "We could not do it. We saw hundreds of soldiers in white uniforms, and we became scared."

Corrie later reflected that "in Africa, soldiers never wear white uniforms. So it must have been angels. What a wonderful thing that the Lord can open the eyes of the enemy so that they see angels!"[7]

Emergency Guidance on the Road

Marlene Wiechman, a 33-year-old mother in West Point, Nebraska, believes angels rendered assistance when her six-year-old daughter's health took a drastic turn for the worse: "Emily had had a stroke at seven months, and she's partially handicapped," Wiechman says. Years later, Emily became ill while the family was vacationing:

> Last year, we went on vacation with my parents to Yellowstone National Park. On the way home, driving through Wyoming, Emily said she didn't feel well. She started vomiting, and her eyes weren't focusing. We needed to get her to a hospital, but the nearest town, Rock Springs, was 70 miles away.

. . . . .

Emily kept getting worse, and as we approached Rock Springs, I prayed we would find help quickly. Just then, we saw a blue-and-white hospital sign. There were three or four more signs that led us straight to the emergency room.[8]

A doctor at the hospital was able to quickly diagnose Emily as having a seizure and was able to stabilize her with anticonvulsants. When the moment of crisis was over, Ms. Wiechman mentioned that the signs had been a lifesaver. "The doctor looked at me and said, 'What signs?' He said he traveled that road every day, and there were no hospital signs. But all four adults in our van had seen them. We went back and looked again. They were gone. I called someone at the chamber of commerce, who said there had never been any hospital signs on that route," Wiechman says. "I believe they were put there for us by God or his angels."[9]

Companion on a Dangerous Mountain

A Christian missionary in Norway believes an angel assisted him on a dangerous mountain.[10] In attempting to reach families living in his valley, he had to descend a dangerous mountain trail. At one steep, dangerous place he stopped to pray, asking God to protect him with His angels. He safely reached the valley without harm.

At the first cottage the missionary met a man and his wife who had been watching his descent of the dangerous trail. "What has become of your companion?" they asked.

"What companion?" the missionary responded.

"The man who was with you," they exclaimed in surprise. "We were watching you as you came down the

. . . . .

mountain, and it really seemed to us that there were two men crossing the mountain together."

"Then," reported the missionary, "I was reminded of my prayer to God for help, and of the word of the Lord in Psalm 34:7, 'The angel of the LORD encampeth round about them that fear him, and delivereth them'" (KJV).

Rescue from a Train Disaster

Bible expositor Arno C. Gaebelein speaks of an incident in which he is convinced an angel sent from God rescued him and his companions from sure disaster. While traveling northward on a train, Gaebelein and his friends committed themselves into God's loving hands for a safe trip. Strangely, they sensed danger in their hearts that night—but they nevertheless trusted in God for safety.

They slept through that night peacefully. The next morning when they awoke they were informed of a near-tragedy that had occurred during the night:

> The train was hours late and the crew told us that near to midnight the train had been flagged by a farmer and had been brought to a stop less than five yards from a deep abyss. A storm further north sent its floodwaters down the creek and washed the wooden bridge away. A farmer was asleep. He said a voice awoke him to arise. He heard the rushing water and hastily dressed himself and lit a lantern, when he heard the oncoming train, which he stopped in time.[11]

Gaebelein has always believed that the voice that awoke the farmer that night was nothing less than an angel of God. He wonders how many other times in his

. . . . .

21

life he has been rescued from danger without even knowing danger was present.

Rescue from a Burning Room

One day in 1977 Linda Gates of Sacramento, California was cleaning her kitchen when she suddenly heard her four-year-old boy Michael running down the hall. She then heard the front door slam shut—an unusual occurrence since the door was warped and required adult strength to close tightly. Upon going outside, Linda found Michael, his eyes wide. He said, "A man got me out, Mama! A man got me out!"

Michael then led his mother to his smoke-filled room, where a curtain was burning. As it turned out, Michael had been playing with a box of matches and set the curtains on fire. After firefighters put out the blaze, one of them told Linda the smoke could easily have killed her son.

Linda recounts, "Michael told me that a man with long blond hair and a 'many-colored' shirt had appeared at his door and said, 'Michael, come out of there.' When my son said he wanted to look for his teddy bear, the man pulled him out of the room."

That evening their bedtime story just happened to be about Daniel and the lions' den. The key verse for the story was, "My God sent his angel, and he shut the mouths of the lions. They have not hurt me, because I was found innocent in his sight" (Daniel 6:22). Linda was confident that God had sent His angel to rescue her son.[12]

God's Heavenly Helpers

Were bona fide angels really involved in each of the above cases? They all have the ring of authenticity to me, but only God knows for sure. One thing is clear, though. Each of the above cases illustrates in a graphic way what Scripture has to say about the role of angels: "Are not all angels ministering spirits sent to serve those who will inherit salvation?" (Hebrews 1:14).

The root meaning of the word "ministering" has to do with rendering service. God created the angels to render service in various capacities. Popular Bible expositor Ray Stedman says that angelic ministry may involve protection (Psalm 91:11), guidance (Genesis 19:16-17), encouragement (Judges 6:12), deliverance (Acts 12:7), supply (Psalm 105:40), enlightenment (Matthew 2:19-20), and empowerment (Luke 22:43).[13]

Later we will see that angels are also involved in other kinds of service not specifically related to Christians. Some angels render service directly to God and Christ. Other angels are involved in bringing judgment against unbelievers. We shall see that angels are involved in carrying out the sovereign bidding of God in many different ways.

Angel sightings are recounted daily, filling talk shows, seminars, and the pages of those best-selling books. One angel story tops the next. Understandable. They're more multi-talented than Bo Jackson. There's no end to what they can do.

Craig Wilson[1]

·2·
Flying High: Angel Popularity on the Rise

There was a time when angels were relegated mainly to Christmas cards and manger scenes. But not anymore. Angels have infiltrated the popular culture—*big time!* Indeed, belief in angels is virtually soaring across the religious spectrum in America—from mainline Christians to New Agers who seek comfort from these heavenly helpers in a troubled and often chaotic world.[2]

Of course, angels have been the subject matter of popular songs for decades. Hit songs in the angel genre include "Earth Angel," "Angel Eyes," "Johnny Angel," "I'm Living Right Next Door to an Angel," "Where Angels Fear to Tread," and "You Are My Special Angel."[3] Malcolm Godwin, in his 1990 book *Angels: An Endangered Species*, estimates that "over the last 30 years one in every 10 pop songs mentions an angel."[4]

In recent years, however, angels have moved from being mentioned metaphorically in pop songs directly into the mainstream of American society. In fact, some of today's biggest magazines are running feature stories—

even *cover* stories—on angels, including *Time, Newsweek, Ladies Home Journal,* and *Redbook.* Moreover, in mid-1994 ABC aired a two-hour, prime-time special entitled *Angels: The Mysterious Messengers,* hosted by Patty Duke. Who would have ever thought that angels would be the subject of a prime-time television program in twentieth-century America?

Angelmania has clearly penetrated Western culture on a broad level. In December of 1993 *Time* magazine put it this way:

> In the past few years [angels] have lodged in the popular imagination, celestial celebrities trailing clouds of glory as they come. There are angels-only boutiques, angel newsletters, angel seminars, angels on *Sonya Live.* A TIME poll indicates that most Americans believe in angels. Harvard Divinity School has a course on angels; Boston College has two. Bookstores have had to establish angel sections. In the most celebrated play on Broadway, Tony Kushner's Pulitzer-prize-winning *Angels in America,* a divine messenger ministers to a man with AIDS. In *Publishers Weekly*'s religious bestseller list, five of the 10 paperback books are about angels.[5]

Newsweek magazine, in a similar tone, asserted in late 1993 that "angels are appearing everywhere in America."[6] The article noted that "those who see angels, talk to them, and put others in touch with them are prized guests on television and radio talk shows. Need inspiration? There are workshops that will assist you in identifying early angel experiences or in unleashing your 'inner angel.' Tired of your old spirit guide? New

Age channelers will connect you with Michael the Archangel. Have trouble recognizing the angels among us? Join an angel focus group."[7]

Redbook magazine gets to the heart of the matter in saying that "angels sell."[8] Indeed, "angel seminars are packed in cities and rural retreats all over the country. In some, participants simply share experiences; others promise that 'getting in touch with your inner angel' will help solve your problems, from relationship woes to addiction. . . . Calendars, postcards, T-shirts, and even angel sunglasses are being churned out at a fiendish pace; there are even collectors' clubs."[9]

In a poll conducted by *Time* in late 1993, a whopping 69 percent of American adults confirmed that they believed in the existence of angels. A full 46 percent acknowledged that they believed they had their own guardian angel. And some 32 percent claimed to have felt an angelic presence at some time in their lives.[10]

Belief in angels is even higher among teenagers. In fact, teen belief in angels has steadily increased from 64 percent in 1978 to 76 percent in 1992, according to Gallup polls. This means that three out of every four young Americans believe in angels today.[11]

Certainly the sudden popularity of angel books has taken the publishing industry by surprise. Phyllis Tickle, religion editor for *Publishers Weekly*, noticed in 1992 that a "small spurt" of books about angels was appearing on the religious bestseller charts. But recently that spurt has become a torrent, "pouring out of every faucet in the publishing business."[12]

Sophy Burnham's *A Book of Angels* opened the floodgates in 1990, and by early 1994 went into its thirtieth printing—with some 566,000 copies in print.[13] A sequel, *Angel Letters*, has 200,000 copies in print. Other authors

have hopped on the angel bandwagon and have published a plethora of bestselling angel books. As reported
by *Newsweek*, these include:

> Joan Wester Anderson's *Where Angels Walk*
> (400,000 copies); *Ask Your Angels*, by Alma
> Daniel, Timothy Wyllie, and Andrew Ramer
> (270,000 copies); Eileen Elias Freeman's
> *Touched by Angels* (65,000); and four New
> Agey angel volumes by Terry Lynn Taylor
> that have a total of 320,000 copies in print.
> And that's only the top of the list. Sparked
> by the renewed interest in angels, pub-
> lishers have reissued two old reliables: phi-
> losopher Mortimer Adler's 1982 scholastic
> analysis, *Angels and Us*, and a revised edi-
> tion of Billy Graham's greatest hit, *Angels:
> God's Secret Agents*, which has sold 2.6 mil-
> lion copies since 1975.[14]

In view of such phenomenal sales, Phyllis Tickle
has concluded that "nineteen ninety-three was clearly
the year of the angels."[15] But the angel craze is not over.
Angel books continue to pour out from publishing
houses faster than anyone can keep up with them. Eileen
Freeman, a well-known angel enthusiast, commented:
"I have about six linear feet of bookshelf space just
devoted to books on angels."[16]

Books are not the only angel merchandise selling
well in America today. There are actually stores that sell
nothing but angel merchandise. An example of this is
Sally Allen's "Angels for All Seasons" store in Denver,
Colorado. The *Los Angeles Times* reports that "her store
opened last September [1993], and did a 'phenomenal'
$150,000 in business the first four months. She is now

planning to open up other shops of angel collectibles in an airport and a mall."[17] According to *Newsweek*, across America there are presently "more than 30 specialty stores and catalog houses devoted exclusively to angel-ware."[18]

Understanding Today's Angel Craze

The question that naturally comes to mind is, *Why* are angels so popular in twentieth-century America? What has given rise to the incredible present-day angel-mania that is sweeping our nation?

Time reports that the "rising fascination is more popular than theological, a grass-roots revolution of the spirit in which all sorts of people are finding all sorts of reasons to seek answers about angels for the first time in their lives. Just what is their nature? Why do they appear to some people and not to others? Do people turn into angels when they die? What role do they play in heaven and on earth?"[19] *Time* notes that "while the questions have the press of novelty, they are as old as civilization, for the idea of angels has hovered about us for ages."[20]

Of course, Christians are excited about angels because angelology is a biblical doctrine—and their interest in angels reflects their *greater* interest in Scripture. Others, however, have become excited about angels because they have bought into wildly *un*biblical ideas about angels. I'll show you what I mean as I touch on some of the various reasons today's "angel experts" suggest for the rise in angel popularity.

• *Angels are popular today because they allegedly offer humankind a form of spirituality that does not involve commitment to God or the laws of God.* As *Time* puts it, "for those who choke too easily on God and his rules . . . angels are the handy compromise, all fluff and meringue, kind, nonjudgmental. And they are available to everyone, like aspirin."[21] *Christianity Today* magazine suggests that "angels too easily provide a temptation for those who want a 'fix' of spirituality without bothering with God himself."[22]

Joan Wester Anderson, author of *Where Angels Walk*, says "angels are a gateway to spirituality for people who find the Judeo-Christian image of God too threatening."[23] Angels offer a form of spirituality devoid of Jesus and God.

Sophy Burnham likewise suggests that the current popularity of angels is "because we have created this concept of God as punitive, jealous, judgmental." She assures us that "angels never are. They are utterly compassionate."[24]

In a similar vein, Eileen Freeman writes:

> Many adults find modern views of God unacceptable or too impersonal, too distant, and do not accept the Christian view that Jesus is God in human, personal, accessible form. Yet the search for God is a part of our inmost being. The need to be united with our Source is universal. It is, as Blaise Pascal the French philosopher put it, the "God-shaped vacuum in the center of every human heart." Such people often see in angels what they cannot yet see in God: personal love reaching out to touch them; ageless wisdom reaching out to enlighten them; incredible power harnessed to inspire them.[25]

Phyllis Tickle says that "like ecology, angels allow us a safe place to talk to each other about spiritual things. They provide a socially acceptable way to talk about God without stating a theological commitment."[26] She adds,

"They're a safe way to say, 'I'm a seeker,' because they lead straight back to every branch of the Abrahamic faith. Islam recognizes them—absolutely. Judaism recognizes them—without question. Christianity—they are inextricably part of the New Testament story."[27]

As well, Tickle says, angels have been made "aesthetically acceptable through the arts, and culturally acceptable through the New Age movement. It's possible to believe in angels without being a kook. They are a way to come back in and test the spiritual waters—a bridge back to Mother Church."[28]

• *Angels are popular today because they are allegedly a means of attaining God's help without having to deal directly with God.* "With angels around, people feel they don't have to bother an Almighty God in order to get help," says Professor Robert Ellwood, a specialist in unorthodox religions at the University of Southern California.[29]

At the First Church of the Angels in Carmel, California, minister Andre D'Angelo calls on angel power to help his clients work out "unresolved traumas." D'Angelo compares God to the CEO of a large corporation: "You can't always get through, but you can always reach a good executive secretary," he reasons. "An angel is like a good executive secretary."[30]

• *Angels are popular today because they have allegedly stepped up their activity among human beings in recent years in order to help them.* Eileen Freeman, in her popular book *Touched by Angels*, suggests:

> For the past two hundred years or so, the angels of God have been increasingly visible in their deeds and actions as powerful forces of good for the human race. In the past fifty years, they have stepped up their work in

. . . . .

our midst; and in the past decade our awareness of angelic activity has increased beyond
anything I believe this world has ever seen.
Not only are people by the thousands re-
porting that their lives have been recently
touched by angels, but many others have
gained the courage to speak of life-trans-
forming events dating back decades earlier,
when an angelic encounter changed the
course of their destiny.[31]

According to the *San Jose Mercury News*, New Age
angel devotees say that "visitations are becoming more
common because the angels recognize how badly humanity needs help in troubled times."[32] Sophy Burnham, the most popular angel author today, says, "They've
come as messengers. . . . We are approaching the millen-
nium. We're at the end of a century that has seen
unbelievable horrors . . . and the angels are saying people
can't be allowed to live like this any longer."[33]

Robert Smith, author of *In the Presence of Angels*, says
"these angels are here more than ever because of our
need, because of the pain we are in, because of the
difficulties we're encountering during this time of transition. The gateways to a new period in history have
opened, bringing forth fresh possibilities for higher consciousness around the world. . . . The angels are here to
help us with that passage and to protect us if all else
fails."[34]

An Associated Press report said "it is no coincidence that angels are becoming more prevalent in an age
when humanity seems to need divine help to solve such
ills as homelessness, hunger, and the destruction of the
environment."[35] Freeman adds, "I think people are
interested because they sense a need as a race and as

individuals for help. . . . Angels care very much about us. They want to help."[36]

• *Guardian angels are popular today because of people's perceived need for protection in an often threatening world.* In a feature article on angels, the *Los Angeles Times* reports that "times have gotten so bad that guardian angels are turning up in individuals' lives with increasing frequency, and people are more receptive to the heavenly beings than ever before."[37]

John Ronner, author of *Do You Have a Guardian Angel?*, says that tough times have helped increase interest in guardian angels. "We're in somewhat troubled times now. . . . People find a great deal of comfort in the thought that something larger than themselves and benevolent may be looking out for them."[38]

"People need protection, and they're scared," says Rabbi Susan Laemmle of the University of Southern California Hillel Center. "They don't have a community, they need friends, and so they're reaching out."[39] Laemmle reflects, "The world is a dangerous place, and anything we can do that will give us a sense of protection is attractive."[40] Many people feel insecure because of rising crime and seemingly insurmountable societal problems, and they believe they have found a means of coping by trusting in guardian angels.

Marv Meyer, a religious studies professor at Chapman University, states, "I think angels are popular now because the ordinary ways of coping are not working. People are lost in the machinery of society and are getting chewed up. So you need someone you can trust, maybe your own guardian angel, someone you can call down yourself."[41]

• *Angels have grown in popularity as a reaction against the materialism and secularism of Western society.* Sophy Burnham says, "I think Americans in the '80s became weary of 20 years of materialism. We were spiritually starved and hungry for some hope and inspiration. I think that's why angels continue to be such a success."[42]

"It's a New Age answer to the hopelessness of secularity," affirms theologian Ted Peters of Pacific Lutheran Theological Seminary in Berkeley, California.[43] Eileen Freeman likewise says, "We've come through a very materialistic period in this country. People are searching for a deeper spirituality."[44]

Many who have cast their lot with the angels say it has become easier to believe in heavenly beings as we see evidence that high technology is limited in its ability to solve societal ills. "Our age is a scientific age," says Marilynn Webber of Marilynn's Angels, a mail-order company in Riverside, California. "We came to realize this didn't get us where we wanted to go so there is more of an interest in spiritual things."[45]

• *Angels are popular today because they are believed to bring meaning and purpose into our lives.* Angel author Terry Lynn Taylor asks, "What happens to us when we ask the angels into our lives? *Life becomes more meaningful.*"[46] She affirms, "These angels 'make life worth living,' so to speak. They provide us with unconditional happiness, fun, and mirth. They also help out with romance and wealth. And they help us extinguish worries that plague our lives."[47]

Taylor says she wrote her book on angels "to share information that has made my life fun, happy, meaningful, exciting, successful, loving, easy to take, and less serious!"[48] She says, "Angels are heaven-sent agents who are always available to help you create heaven in your life."[49]

• *Angels are popular today because they allegedly give assurance to all people regarding life after death.* Critic Harold Bloom says, "The interest in angels is about not wanting to die."[50] In their encounters with angels, "human beings gain experimental assurance that they, too, have a heavenly home."[51]

Sophy Burnham affirms that "we need not be afraid to die. . . . That we do not die! This I have learned. This much I have seen with my own eyes." The angels have told her so.[52]

Impostors Among Us?

By now I think you can see what I mean when I say that the excitement many have about angels today is rooted in wildly unbiblical ideas. We shall touch on even *wilder* pespectives about angels in the next chapter. It will become increasingly clear that much of the angel craze presently sweeping our nation has little to do with the heavenly helpers described in the pages of the Bible.

In fact, much of what is being taught about angels today in some of the bestselling books would seem to have more to do with *fallen* angels (demons) than God's holy angels. These fallen angels are nothing but impostors who pose as benevolent helpers of humankind yet in reality foster a spirituality without Christ and without God (2 Corinthians 11:14-15).

. . . . .

Another way to hail an angel . . .
is to color-coordinate your wardrobe.
According to this somewhat far-out
idea, soft green clothes will lure in
guardian angels of the home, and deep
sapphire blue will get the attention
of healing angels.

—John Ronner[1]

·3·

Celestial Quackery

A 1993 cover story about angels and angel books in *Newsweek* magazine acutely observed, "If the first wave of books brought angels—and their believers—out of the culture closet, the second wave is even more ambitious. With subtitles like 'A handbook for aspiring angels' and 'The angels' guide to personal growth,' they signal a move from telling stories to *making contact*."[2]

Making contact with angels! It seems almost inconceivable that this would become a matter of great interest to Americans in the twentieth century. But indeed, it *has* become a matter of interest—and in a very big way. We can hardly keep up with the seemingly endless flow of books that set forth different methods and ideas about how to make contact with angels. And, as we will see, many of these methods and ideas involve mysticism and various forms of occultism.

Making Contact with Angels

The mystical element is evident in that a number of today's angel writers speak of the need for "intuition" that enables us to sense the presence of angels. For example, Terry Lynn Taylor, author of *Messengers of Light: The Angels' Guide to Spiritual Growth*, says that "to get to know angels, it helps if you can transcend the 'seeing is believing' paradigm and adopt an open mind and a stance of 'knowing by intuition.'"[3]

Taylor says the main source of her ideas about angels was her own intuition: "The main source I used for the book was my strongest intuitions regarding angels. . . .And, of course, I asked the angels to inspire me at all times."[4]

It is no wonder, then, that there is such a wide diversity of strange ideas floating around out there about angels. When people depart from the objective truth recorded in God's Word—the Bible—and replace it with mystical intuition, the door is wide open for new ideas to come from "the other side."

What about occultism? Alma Daniel, Timothy Wyllie, and Andrew Ramer—in their book *Ask Your Angels*, published by Ballantine Books (a major publisher)—say that techniques used to contact angels include Eastern meditation, visualization, breath control, exercises with chakras (alleged energy centers in the body), tuning into angel frequencies, channeling, and divination.[5]

Jane Howard, in her book *Commune with the Angels*, likewise says that "through [Eastern] meditation, prayer, and psychic development exercises, we can become fluent in seeing, hearing, and sensing members of other kingdoms. When we use our superphysical sense of sight to develop our clairvoyance, we are able to see the angels face to face."[6]

In the pages ahead we will examine these and other occultic methods for contacting angels. Along the way, you will come to see that its title—"Celestial Quackery"—is not an exaggeration.

. . . . .

Please note that in this chapter I will *not* be setting forth a thorough Christian response to each of the strange ideas mentioned (though I will occasionally cite a Bible verse to refute an idea). We will look at the biblical view of angels in chapters 4 through 14.[7]

Channeling

Alma Daniel, Timothy Wyllie, and Andrew Ramer say channeling is one of the best means for making angel contact. In their book they make an analogy using a television set, and ask us to imagine that we *are* the set: "There are many channels or stations broadcasting. (In this case, channel refers to a voice, not to the person receiving it.) Until you open to the angels, the only channel you're likely to get on your set comes from your mind, from your ego. . . .Once you tune into the angels, you may find yourself receiving other stations as well—voices of guides, extraterrestrials, and nature spirits."[8]

These authors claim to present the wisdom of Abigrael, a genderless angelic being who allegedly gives them instructions via channeling.[9] And just as they themselves have made angel contact through channeling, so also do they now seek to help others do this through their book and their New Age workshops.[10]

Other New Agers claim the ability to act as a channel so you can communicate with (and gain wisdom from) your guardian angel. Ann Daniel, of the New Covenant Center in Denver, Colorado, says "your guardian angel knows more about you than you even know about yourself. Help may be only a step away."[11]

Daniel uses channeling to get in touch with a counselee's guardian angel so that wisdom may be provided to him or her. She calls her sessions "angel listenings."[12]

A typical angel listening lasts somewhere between 20 and 30 minutes, and is really nothing more than a

. . . . .

conversation between the counselee and his or her angel speaking through Ann. The listening begins with a prayer "to protect us from bad angels (sent by Satan) and to guide us to the right interpretation of the angel's message."[13]

Following the prayer, Ann meditates for a few moments and puts herself into a kind of trance whereby she is able to communicate with the angel. Using a pencil and pad, she writes everything the angel relays to her. The counselee never actually hears the angel speaking, though some people have claimed to see a glow of light or sense a presence in the room.[14] Through this channeling experience, counselees are said to receive from their guardian angels specific instructions and wisdom on a variety of issues.

From a biblical perspective, however, all forms of channeling are off-limits for the Christian. Indeed, God detests channelers and spiritists: "Let no one be found among you . . . who is a medium or spiritist or who consults the dead. Anyone who does these things is detestable to the LORD" (Deuteronomy 18:10-12). Scripture also states that "Satan himself masquerades as an angel of light" (2 Corinthians 11:14). Hence he is perfectly capable of impersonating benevolent angels—and he does so to lead people astray. *Angel enthusiasts beware!*

Prayer

Many of today's angel authors say angel contact often comes through prayer. Terry Lynn Taylor is representative in saying that "prayer is a way to communicate with the angels."[15] She advises, "Prayer is the way we talk to angels . . . .When you pray to the angels, pray as if 'it is already done'; in other words, thank the angels in advance for taking care of your burdens."[16] (Notice that she speaks of prayer that is directed *toward angels* and not to God, which directly violates scriptural instructions on prayer—*see* Matthew 6:9.)

Supposedly, angels can also make sure that whenever you choose to pray to God, your prayers will actually reach Him. Jane Howard admonishes, "If you are someone who is concerned about God hearing your prayer 'down here,' trust in the angels' messenger service for a quick delivery of your prayer to God."[17]

Meditation

Terry Lynn Taylor offers advice on how to contact angels via meditation: "Let your attention focus on angels. At this point, you may want to use the word *angel* as a form of mantra [a word that is mystically chanted over and over again]. Allow the word to take you wherever it will. Let a smile come over you, and notice the feeling of peace that comes with it. As you smile, feel yourself lifted and surrounded by white light. Ask the angels to lift you into heaven so that you can meet them."[18]

In his book *In the Presence of Angels*, Robert C. Smith points out the alleged benefit of such meditation: "As we practice withdrawing our attention from the physical world and focusing it on the spiritual, our perception becomes less limited to materiality. The nonphysical realm becomes more real to us, and we develop the mental habit of *attentiveness* to it."[19] Smith later adds, "The tendency of material concerns [interferes] with our receptivity to the angelic realm."[20]

In a similar vein, Jane Howard exhorts us: "Angels are always on call, and meditation is one of the best ways by which we can commune with them. Through meditation we can actually 'call up' the angels. Their number is listed and it's not a costly exchange. It's free and accessible to all, twenty-four hours a day."[21]

. . . . .

Now, I need to emphasize that the meditation described above is not *biblical* meditation. Biblical meditation—in contrast to the mysticism and emptying of the mind that is characteristic of Eastern meditation—involves objective contemplation and deep reflection on God's Word (Joshua 1:8) as well as His Person and faithfulness (Psalm 119; cf. 19:14; 48:9; 77:12; 104:34; 143:5).

New Age Visualization

The popular angel author Sophy Burnham uses guided imagery (or visualization) to help her workshop attendees make contact with angels. As reported in *Newsweek* magazine, "in a typical workshop, like one conducted for 100 aspirants at the Episcopal National Cathedral in Washington, D.C., Burnham uses the conventional techniques of 'guided meditation' to silence the mind and unlock the imagination. Once they'd settled into their personal sacred spaces, her initiates—a third of whom had already experienced angels—were invited to listen for messages."[22]

Jane Howard, who also conducts angel workshops, describes a typical visualization exercise for making angel contact:

> In your mind's eye see a bridge appear before you—a bridge of light. Get up and walk across this bridge that leads you into the angelic realm. Don't be just a spectator and see yourself walking across the bridge—actually *feel* and *imagine* it as you get up and walk. Focus your awareness on walking across the bridge and, if you need to, say to yourself, "I am walking across the bridge with my Guardian Angel." Once on the other side of the bridge acknowledge that

you have crossed over into the angelic realm.[23]

The Christian, of course, recognizes the danger of such guided imagery sessions. For one thing, man's imagination has been thoroughly marred by sin (Genesis 6:5; Romans 8:7; Ephesians 4:18). Beyond this, we must recognize that guided imagery can induce an altered state of consciousness that can have extremely dangerous consequences. The fact is, *any* kind of activity that leads to an altered state of consciousness can make a person vulnerable to demonic affliction.

New Age Crystals

Jane Howard tells us that a "cherubic crystal" can be of great benefit for a person seeking contact with angels. "A cherubic crystal is one that you have activated in meditation and which has been charged by the Cherubim,"[24] she says. Here's what to do after you obtain a suitable crystal:

> Once you have selected the crystal, hold it between the palms of your hands. Ask out loud for the wisdom vibration emanated by the Cherubim to flow through you and into your hands so that the stone will become charged with the Cherubim's vibration. Prepare the crystal once in this manner and you will never have to do it again, unless someone tampers with it or changes its programming.[25]

Howard says that when she holds her cherubic crystal, she can feel it become warm as it is being "charged" and "blessed" by angels. She goes on to say that you can even use a number of "activated crystals" to work with the "different choirs" of the angelic realm.[26]

Of course, there is nothing wrong with a Christian owning a crystal *per se*. After all, crystals are just rocks that God created. However, the New Age use of crystals as described above is sheer occultism and stands condemned by God (Deuteronomy 18:10-12).

Writing Letters

As hard as it may seem to believe, a number of New Age angel authors suggest that a great way of communicating with angels is through writing letters to them. According to Daniel, Wyllie, and Ramer—authors of *Ask Your Angels*—all you have to do is "date your letter, write 'Dear Angel,' and just let your words flow. Ask for your angel's support and/or guidance and give thanks for its assistance in advance. Then sign it at the end as you would a letter to a friend."[27]

Once the letter is completed, it can be placed in your Bible, a meditation altar, or a personal box where special items are kept. The letter may even be put under your pillow. Or, perhaps, you may want to burn the letter, "sending the message up to the heavens with the rising smoke."[28] Regardless of which method you choose, you may rest assured that the letter has been "sent."

Some angel writers, such as Terry Lynn Taylor, suggest that if you are having interpersonal problems with a particular person, you may want to consider writing that person's guardian angel a letter: "If there is someone in your life—your boss, your spouse, your child, your coworker, or your friend—with whom you have trouble communicating without disagreements and arguments over trivial issues, try writing to that person's guarding angel and ask that the situation be understood on the highest level."[29] You can be confident that "when you write to someone else's guardian, the message gets delivered on the angelic level."[30]

Have you ever felt the need to communicate with someone who has died and passed on to the "other side"? If yes, why not write a letter to that person's angel? By so doing (we are told), you can communicate with the dead![31]

If you are not up to writing someone else's guardian angel, don't worry! You can simply "write to your own guardian angel with a request to speak to the other person's guardian angel so you can reach understanding on a deeper level."[32] This keeps things nice and personal.

Daniel, Wyllie, and Ramer assure us that angels are fully capable of communicating back to us through letters. How so? you ask. All you need to do is "pick up another piece of paper . . . . This time, start your letter by writing 'Dear _____,' and fill in your own name. Then relax and let your angel's words come through you in the form of a letter."[33] In other words, you can act as a "channel" through whom your guardian angel can write a letter to you. (In occultic circles this type of practice is known as "automatic handwriting.")

Wearing the Right Colors

John Ronner, author of *Do You Have a Guardian Angel?* tells us that "another way to hail an angel . . . is to color-coordinate your wardrobe. According to this somewhat far-out idea, soft green clothes will lure in guardian angels of the home, and deep sapphire blue will get the attention of healing angels, for example."[34]

In a similar vein, Terry Lynn Taylor tells us in *Messengers of Light* that guardian angels like rose or pink and soft green; healing angels like deep sapphire blue; seraphim angels like crimson red; cherubim angels like blue; the archangel Michael likes deep green, vivid blue, gold, and rose; and Gabriel is attracted to tans, browns, and dark greens.[35] By wearing specific colors, you supposedly can attract specific kinds of angels into your life.

Angelic Appearances Today

Assuming that a person is successful in using one of the above unbiblical methods to make contact with an angel, the question that arises is, What form does that contact take? In examining the New Age pop literature permeating the marketplace today, it would seem (contrary to the explicit teachings of Scripture) that angel appearances can take an incredibly wide variety of forms.

Sophy Burnham says angels can appear "as animals and human beings, with wings or without, male or female, as visions or voices, as that little whisper at your shoulder saying, 'Don't go down that road.' "[36] They can take the form of nudgings, intuition, or coincidence.[37] They can appear as light on the water, or in clouds and rainbows.[38] Burnham says she once saw an angel appear in the form of a swan.[39]

Popular angel writer Eileen Freeman says,

> Angels come to help and guide us in as many guises as there are people who need their assistance. Sometimes we see their ethereal, heavenly shadow, bright with light and radiance. Sometimes we only feel their nearness or hear their whisper. And sometimes they look no different from ourselves— until, their work done, they leave suddenly, quietly, with only a hint of halo or a wisp of wing behind to make us wonder.[40]

. . . . .

Commenting on how angels may be behind intu-ition or nudgings, Marilyn Achiron, in an article in *People Weekly,* writes,

> At certain moments, we feel the irresist-ible impulse to be cautious. Or we might feel a push to proceed. This feeling has been dubbed hunch, intuition, or premonition. Many a person, however, insists such help-ful spiritual intervention is the work of the angels, believing without qualification in heavenly visitors.[41]

John Ronner likewise says, "That sudden surge of confidence, flash of insight, sharp twinge of conscience—may sometimes be coming from a subtly-working angel."[42] Terry Lynn Taylor adds, "Have you ever had an idea just pop into your mind? You have probably had the experi-ence of saying, 'It just dawned on me' or, 'It came to me in a daydream.' Well, those were probably the times your personal angel creativity minister called on you."[43]

Robert Smith calls this type of angel manifestation an "unworded internal realization." He says this includes instances in which a person receives "insight into a problem he or she had been concerned about, a sudden new perspective on a situation, inspiration to follow a specific course of action, or an intuitive hunch that was later shown to be true."[44]

It is also possible, we are told, for an angel appear-ance to be subtly disguised in everyday events. Terry Lynn Taylor therefore urges us to "pay attention to the subtleties in life." She says,

> Angels have many ways of reaching you, but often you miss them. For example, a child,

in a moment of spontaneity, may blurt out a statement for which only you know the meaning. While thumbing through a book, a page may fall open with a clear message in the print. Headlines in the newspaper, taken out of context, might contain your message. Angels with messages often appear to us in dreams. Angels are very creative in the ways they communicate with us; we have to be just as creative when we listen for our messages.[45]

Angel author Jane Howard claims an angel once communicated to her through the lyrics of a song she heard on the radio:

I felt directed by my angel to turn on the radio. When I did, I heard a song which up until that moment had been unknown to me. The chorus of the song contained the words, "I am going to be your soul provider." I felt the words touch my heart and give me the reassurance that no matter what was uncertain in my life, I was going to have the support and love of my Guardian Angel. Together, we would be able to face anything.[46]

Now, one might wonder what cosmic precept governs the particular form an angel appearance might take in regard to a specific person. Joan Wester Anderson, in her bestselling book *Where Angels Walk*, says that "angels have typically appeared in whatever form the visited person was most willing to accept—perhaps a winged version for children, or a benign grandfatherly type for a woman in distress."[47]

. . . . .

Sophy Burnham suggests, "These visitations and insights usually accord with the upbringing and conditioning of the recipient."[48] The rule, she says, is that people receive only as much information as they can bear, *in the form they can stand to hear it*.[49] Indeed, angel appearances seem to "take whatever form the visited person is *willing to accept*; and sometimes no form at all— a dream, a thought, a surge of power, a sense of guidance. They don't seem far removed from natural events. This explains why angels are easily explained away."[50]

Angelic Messages

Regardless of what form an angelic appearance may take, we are told that the messages from angels are always positive. Indeed, Sophy Burnham says the typical message from an angel is, "Don't be afraid, everything is just fine. There is nothing but love."[51] "Things are going to work out," is the constant theme of angel communication.[52]

Beyond this, Terry Lynn Taylor suggests that the "angels' primary concern is to help transform human attitudes toward the positive, lighter side of life."[53] Taylor says, "The main lesson the angels have for us is that we are love, we are God on earth, and it is time to love ourselves and open our hearts."[54] Moreover, angels "are always trying to get through to us with messages designed to bring us into alignment with our higher selves."[55]

Jane Howard similarly says the angels want to "bring us the message of our true identity." She says:

> We are one with 'all that is,' the seen and the unseen. . . . They would show us that we are one with the wind, one with the sun, one with the flowers; that we are one with the angels themselves and one with God.[56]

The Aftereffects of Angelic Visitations

Angels *do* make themselves known, New Age angel enthusiasts assure us. And one way to tell whether you have encountered an angel has to do with the *aftereffects* of angelic visitations. Burnham, for example, says that a key mark of an angelic visitation is that it "brings a calm and peaceful serenity that descends sweetly over you, and this is true even when the angel is not seen."[57]

Burnham also says angels "always leave certain physical manifestations in their wake, something substantive to indicate that what witnesses have seen or felt was not just their imaginations. This may be as slight as a gladdening of the heart or a tingling in the fingertips."[58]

Daniel, Wyllie, and Ramer agree, suggesting that "feelings of love, of greater self-acceptance, of inner peace, of being deeply cared for and recognized, are signs of angelic connection."[59] Even if a person doesn't see anything tangible, angelic presence can allegedly be detected by the presence of the above feelings.

Terry Lynn Taylor goes so far as to suggest that "angels sometimes leave a fragrant scent around for us to smell. . . . Two floral scents they especially like are rose and jasmine."[60] So, if you come across either of these scents in the course of your daily business, Taylor would say you may have encountered an angel.

Alleged Benefits of Angelic Contact

According to the current New Age literature on angels, there are all kinds of benefits to angel contact. One angel enthusiast assures us that people can get guidance from angels, develop close friendships with them, get answers to important questions from them, learn to meditate better with their help, enlist their assistance in times of need, receive their help when going on

. . . . .

a diet, develop angel healing groups in which humans get healed,[61] and much more. The benefits are seemingly endless. Let us now look at some of them in greater detail (and witness "celestial quackery" at its worst).

Angels as "Brain Program Editors"

Angels are believed to help our emotional and psychological state by functioning as brain program editors. Terry Lynn Taylor explains: "Brain program editors, if you allow them, can have access to your brain and mind. They can go into your brain like technicians and improve your programming. If you put yourself in a receptive state, these angels will reprogram your brain by adding new information and discarding negative and stale programs."[62]

Taylor further states that "brain program editors are tiny angels of light that have access to cells and neurotransmitters [in our brains] if we allow them to. They can help us transform negative beliefs to positive ones and 'addicted' cells to free cells."[63] Hence, angels are immensely practical because they can literally change the way we think!

Angels Can Help Us Evolve

According to Eileen Freeman, "the ancient servants of God and humanity [i.e., angels] have a mission, a God-given plan to help us grow in wisdom and love, not just so that we will survive as a race, but so we will be able to grow into what we were always intended to be— perfected beings capable of incredible energies and immense, transforming love."[64]

In some ways, then, it would seem that angels are similar to what New Agers call "Ascended Masters"—

dead, historical persons who have allegedly super-evolved and "ascended" to a higher plane of existence from where they now help us evolve. They also seem similar to what New Agers call "space brothers"—extraterrestrials who are working to help humanity enter into a new time of transformation coming upon the planet.

Angels Can Help Us with Goals

New Age angel enthusiasts say we can team up with angels to accomplish our goals in life.[65] This can be done in any number of different ways. For example, we can make a "declaration" to angels that will help bring about what we desire in life: "Making a declaration to the angels means that you are openly announcing what you want known to heaven. Declaring your goals and statements of things to come will establish a plan of action with the angels . . . . The angels will bless the declaration and add higher inspiration and aspirations to it."[66] I don't know about you, but to me this sounds like a celestial form of "positive confession"—that is, angel-assisted "name it and claim it."

Another way of attaining goals is by holding an angel conference. "Calling a conference with the angels is a way to plan for your future, to define what you want to accomplish, and to recognize key people in your life. Angels act as your consultants and your staff of employees."[67] This supposed role of angels helping people to accomplish their goals is no doubt a key reason for the current popularity of angels in the West.

Angels Can Heal Us

Sol Ta Triane asks, "Did you know angels are the source of physical, mental, and emotional healing energies?

. . . . .

I was able to see that this was true years ago when I developed clairvoyance, the ability to see the angels and also other subtle beings."[68] Do you need a healing in your life? If so, Triane believes angels can fulfill your need.

Terry Lynn Taylor agrees:

> Basically, all angels are healers as well as messengers....They can also rearrange your cells on a microscopic level, with the help of your own imagination. Visualize angels programming your immune system with healing messages and charging it up with energy.[69]

Angels Can Bring Us Comfort

Sophy Burnham tells us that if we trust angels, they will "comfort us with invisible warm hands, and always they try to give us what we want."[70] As well, the angels can function as a cheering squad for our higher selves. "These angels cheer with little voices, 'Don't give up.... We like who you are.... Everything's going to be okay.... We are proud of you.'"[71]

Angels can also help us deal with death—including the death of a pet. According to one account, an elderly lady had to take her cat to the vet. "Unfortunately, the cat needed to be put to sleep. The lady sat in the waiting room and looked out the window. She saw her cat in the arms of an angel. The angel had the face of a cat and looked at the cat with sheer love and care. Cradling the cat gently, the angel ascended. The lady watched until they were out of sight."[72]

Angels also assist us in helping friends through the gateway of death. Daniel, Wyllie, and Ramer offer this advice:

. . . . .

If you are close to someone who is about to leave the physical plane, you can work with your angel and the guardian of your friend or relation to help that person approach death with more peace of mind, knowing that this is the next step in the journey of evolution. Ask the angels to help you understand the needs of your friend on an empathic level.[73]

Daniel, Wyllie, and Ramer explain that "our culture perpetuates the notion that life is short, death is forever, and something to be feared. That isn't the angelic view. They tell us that we are immortal souls, who keep evolving, even after death."[74]

Angels and Twelve-Step Programs

Angel enthusiasts say that "from [the angel's] point of view, the twelve steps make a lot of sense. Angels are especially pleased with the fact that many people find their way back to their spiritual path through twelve-step programs, and begin to lead the happy and successful lives they were meant to live."[75]

Now, step two in the 12-step program says, "We came to believe that a *power greater than ourselves* could restore us to sanity" (emphasis added). Angels can be that greater power, we are told: "Begin to repeat: 'I am not alone; the love of the angels is with me at all times.'"[76] You should "repeat positive affirmations whenever you feel alone, and ask the angels to give you a sign that they are with you. You are not alone!"[77]

Angels and a Higher Consciousness

Eileen Freeman, author of *Touched by Angels*, explains that "the angels are among us to help raise our consciousness." She explains:

. . . . .

The angels are among us to help raise our consciousness, our spiritual awareness as a race, not just as individuals....The whole earth is hovering on the edge of a transformation so glorious that we have no idea how to describe it. The angels are among us as guides, to help us through and into a new level of consciousness on earth. And in time, we will come to see the angels who were all around us all the time and live with them as friends and helpers.[78]

Freeman claims that beginning in 1979 and for three years afterward, she received intuitions and "heart-to-heart communications" from her own guardian angel. This angel allegedly told her that about 250 years ago, many of the angels who are guardians to the human race entered into a new way of working with select human beings.[79]

These angels and humans are said to be "covenanted together to live in a much closer and more obvious spiritual relationship than most humans do, in order to become a leaven among all, for the transformation of the world."[80] Freeman says,

The idea is not that a few privileged become an exclusive club, but that angel and human act as hubs or nuclei around the world, with the aim that in time, all people and their guardian angels will share such close relationships. There's nothing magical or superstitious about it. It's not a private pipeline to God. It's simply another means by which God bestows grace upon us.[81]

. . . . .

Angels as "Copilots"

We are told that angels are ready and willing to function as "copilots" of our lives. Terry Lynn Taylor explains that "if you ever need them to take over, they are ready and capable. . . .Copilots act as your invisible secretaries, arranging and ordering your days so that you don't have to make extra trips, reminding you about appointments and deadlines you are about to miss in your confusion."[82] Taylor thus urges people to "let go and let angels."[83]

Angels and New Religious Experiences

Some angel writers believe that when a new angelic guide comes into your life, you may find yourself with a desire to learn about a particular culture or religion that was previously foreign to your experience. "You start buying books, artifacts, incense, music, or clothes that will teach you the essence of this new interest and its spiritual offerings."[84]

If, for example, one of your angelic spiritual guides is a Native American, you may find yourself having visions that put you in touch with Mother Earth. You may then end up having a greater respect for planet earth.[85]

Michael the archangel is said to be a strong proponent of free thinking, and he supposedly encourages this in humans. "Michael sends us inspiration that urges us to open our minds to new ways of thinking and encourages us to figure out for ourselves where we need to be and how to get there. Creating our own religion can help us free our thinking and figure things out for ourselves. Think about ways the angels can help you form your own religion in a fun and humorous way."[86] (The *biblical* Michael, in contrast to this New Age impostor, is always seen doing the bidding of the only true God—*see* Daniel 10:13-21; 12:1; Jude 9.)

Angels and Our Views of God

New Age angel "experts" tell us we need to follow the angels' examples by getting rid of our limiting concepts of God. "Angels do not care what name you give to God, or what gender you assign to God; the basic common denominator they respond to is simply that *God is love.*"[87]

Taylor explains that "instead of thinking about God as a parental figure, an object of my demands, a force that could give me what I wanted if the conditions were proper, I came to see my role as God's partner in creating the things I want....The angels helped me arrive at this realization."[88] In other words, the angels helped Taylor reformulate God in her own mind—a God that was *to her own liking.*

For this reason, Taylor is careful to warn her readers not to get uptight when she uses the term "God":

> Don't let the word "God" scare you or turn you off. If necessary, whenever you see God mentioned in this book, substitute a term that makes you feel more comfortable, such as "the Universe," "Mother Nature," "the Great Spirit," or whatever name puts you in touch with a higher power. Just keep in mind that angels belong to a living higher order, which they work and play to maintain.[89]

Looking Ahead

In this chapter we have examined a plethora of strange ideas about God's heavenly helpers—and we've

. . . . .

only touched upon the tip of the iceberg. *There is so much more we could talk about*, but space forbids. In any event, I think you can see why I've titled this chapter "Celestial Quackery."

Beginning in the next chapter, we will focus our attention on what *Scripture* tells us about angels—what they are like and what they do in God's universe. John Calvin, the great Reformer who himself wrote about angels, said, "We should not indulge in speculations concerning the angels, but search out the witness of Scripture."[90] I agree with Calvin wholeheartedly.

I will be approaching the rest of this book with one fundamental assumption in mind: The Bible—God's Word—is the *only authoritative source* from which we can derive knowledge about angels and other spiritual matters. God is the creator of angels (Colossians 1:16), and it is He who tells us all that we need to know about them.

PART 2

What Angels
Are Like

. . . . , . . .

Praise him, all his angels,
praise him, all his heavenly hosts. . . .
Let them praise the name of the LORD,
for he commanded and they were created.

—Psalm 148:2,5

·4·

The Origin of Angels

The Bible has a lot to say about angels. The New Testament speaks of them some 165 times; the Old Testament, just over 100 times. Of course, even if the Bible mentioned angels just once, that would be enough for us to accept the doctrine as true. But because there are hundreds of such references, "angelology" (as theologians call it) is obviously an important doctrine for us to understand.[1]

It is significant that angels are not confined to just one period of Bible history. Nor are they found in just a few books of the Bible. In fact, angels are mentioned in 34 different Bible books, from the earliest (whether you think Genesis or Job was written first) to the last—the book of Revelation.[2] The existence and activity of angels is prominently displayed all throughout the scriptural witness.

But where did angels come from? Have they been around forever, or did they come into being at a point in time? And if they came into being at a point in time, *why*, *when,* and *how* did that happen? It is to these questions that we now turn our attention.

Angels Are Created Beings

Some angelologists (people who study the doctrine of angels) have proposed that every new wish or desire that God expresses automatically brings into existence a new angel whose sole mission is to accomplish that wish or desire. It has been suggested that the lifespan of some of these angels is limited to the duration of their specific duty or service to God. Once they finish their task, they die.[3]

Others have set forth the idea that humans become angels at the moment of death. As soon as a person dies, so it is believed, he or she becomes an angel. This idea has been popularized in a number of Hollywood motion pictures in recent years.

Both of the above ideas are patently unbiblical. As we observed in chapter 3, the Bible—God's Word—is the *only authoritative source* from which we can derive knowledge about angels and other spiritual matters. And as we consult God's Word, one thing becomes abundantly clear: *Angels are created beings.* They have not existed forever. Nor were they formerly humans. They were created *as angels.*

In Psalm 148:2-5 we read the following words of worship and praise:

> Praise him, *all his angels,*
>   praise him, *all his heavenly hosts.*
> Praise him, sun and moon,
>   praise him, all you shining stars.
> Praise him, you highest heavens
>   and you waters above the skies.

. . . . .

Let them praise the name of the LORD,
  for he commanded and they were created
  (emphasis added).

This passage clearly affirms that God spoke the word and the angels were instantly created. They came into being at a specific point in time.

God's Word also indicates that angels were created as *permanent* beings; they are not portrayed as passing out of existence upon completion of a particular duty for God. Michael, for example, is pictured as an angelic servant of God in Daniel 12 (hundreds of years before Christ's incarnation) *as well as* in Revelation 12 (in the end times). Michael, like all other angels, is a *permanent spirit being*.

Now, God is consistently portrayed as the Creator throughout the Old Testament. When we get to the New Testament, however, we are explicitly told that Jesus Christ was the actual agent of creation. This, of course, is a clear indication of Christ's deity. For it is *as God* that Christ brought the universe into being (John 1:3; Colossians 1:16; Hebrews 1:2,10; cf. Isaiah 44:24). Let us briefly consider what Scripture tells us about Christ's work as Creator.

John 1:3—All Things Were Made by Christ

John's Gospel tells us, "In the beginning was the Word, and the Word was with God, and the Word was God. He was with God in the beginning. Through him all things were made; without him nothing was made that has been made" (John 1:1-3).

How the apostle John must have exulted as he walked by Jesus' side, knowing that next to him stood the Creator of the universe in all of its vastness! Surely he must have marveled at how the stars above him were the

. . . . .

handiwork of his friend, companion, and Savior, Jesus Christ. No wonder John had such a worshipful attitude toward Jesus (John 1:14; 2:11; 20:30-31).

Notice that John states Christ's creative work both positively and negatively: *positively*, "through him all things were made"; *negatively*, "without him nothing was made that has been made" (John 1:3). That John states this truth in both ways is significant, for he wanted the reader to fully grasp that Christ Himself is the sovereign Creator of all things—including the entire angelic realm.

How did Christ carry out His creative work? The Scriptures are clear that He merely gave the command and the universe leapt into existence. Scripture also indicates that when Christ did the work of creation, He did so in an instantaneous fashion. Psalm 33 tells us, "By the word of the LORD were the heavens made; and all the host of them by the breath of His mouth . . . . For He spake, and it was done; he commanded, and it stood fast" (verses 6,9 (KJV cf. Genesis 1:3,6,9,14,20,24).

Hebrews 11:3 likewise tells us that "the universe was formed at God's command." John Whitcomb comments that "it is quite impossible to imagine a time interval in the transition from nonexistence to existence! 'And God said, Let there be light: and there was light' (Genesis 1:3). At one moment there was no light; the next moment there was!"[4] Similarly, at one moment there was no angelic realm; the next moment there was!

It is important to understand that the angels apparently were *all* created *simultaneously*. As theologian Louis Berkhof puts it, "Their full number was created in the beginning; there has been no increase in their ranks"[5] (*see* Hebrews 12:22 and Revelation 5:11). Unlike human beings, who are conceived and born at different times in history, all of the angels were created *at a single moment*.

. . . . .

Matthew 22:30 would seem to support this, for there we read that angels do not marry and thus do not have children.[6]

Colossians 1:16—Christ Created the Angels

In keeping with John's testimony, the apostle Paul affirms that by Christ "all things were created: things in heaven and on earth, visible and invisible, whether thrones or powers or rulers or authorities; all things were created by him and for him. He is before all things, and in him all things hold together" (Colossians 1:16-17).

The little phrase "all things" means that Christ created the whole universe of things. "Every form of matter and life owes its origin to the Son of God, no matter in what sphere it may be found, or with what qualities it may be invested....Christ's creative work was no local or limited operation; it was not bounded by this little orb [earth]."[7] Everything—whether it be simple or complex, visible or invisible, heavenly or earthly, immanent or transcendent—is the product of Christ.

It is highly revealing that Paul says that Christ created "thrones," "powers," "rulers," and "authorities." In the rabbinic (Jewish) thought of the first century, these words were used to describe different orders of angels (*see* Romans 8:38; Ephesians 1:21; 3:10; 6:12; Colossians 2:10,15). Apparently there was a heresy flourishing in Colossae (the city in which the Colossian church was located) that involved the worship of angels. In this worship, Christ had been degraded. So, to correct this grave error, Paul emphasizes in Colossians 1:16 that Christ is the One who created all things—*including all the angels*—and hence, He is supreme and is alone worthy to be worshiped.[8]

Paul also states of Christ that "all things were created by him and *for* him" (Colossians 1:16b, emphasis

. . . . .

added). Creation is "for" Christ in the sense that He is the end for which all things exist. They are meant to serve His will, to contribute to His glory. "Christ is outside creation, prior to it, distinct from it, and He is sovereign to it all, for it was created by Him and indeed *for* Him."[9]

Hence, angels were created—as were all other things—to serve and glorify Christ, not to act according to their own wills or independently of God. This Christ-centered aspect of angels is almost never mentioned in the current bestselling literature on angels.

When Were the Angels Created?

Granting that angels are created beings, a question that has consistently been debated for many centuries has to do with *when* they were created. More specifically, were they created at the same time as planet earth, or at some time prior to the creation of earth?

Saint Augustine commented that when Scripture speaks of the creation, it is not plainly stated *when* the angels were created, "but if mention is made, it is implicit under the name of 'heaven,' when it is said, 'In the beginning God created the heavens and the earth.'"[10] In other words, Augustine assumed the angels were created when the heavens were created.

Many theologians down through the centuries have suggested that the angels were created some time prior to the creation of the earth—and I think there is good evidence to support this view. Job 38:7, for example, makes reference to the "sons of God" (KJV) singing at the time the earth was created. Many scholars believe these "sons of God" in Job 38 are angels.[11] After all, the term "sons of God" is used elsewhere in Job in reference to angels (Job 1:6; 2:1 KJV). (We will discover *why* angels are called "sons of God" in chapter 7.)

. . . . .

James Montgomery Boice is representative of contemporary Bible scholars in saying that "if Job 38:7 is to be taken as referring to angels, as there is every reason for it to be, then even before the creation of the material universe [the planets and stars] there was a vast world of spirit beings."[12] These angelic spirit beings sang as a massive choir when God created the earth. What a moment that must have been!

"Elect" and "Evil" Angels

It is important to grasp that *all* the angels in God's universe were originally created good and holy, just as God made and pronounced all His creation good (Genesis 1:31; 2:3). Jude 6 affirms that originally *all* the angels were holy creatures. It is inconsistent with the holy character of God that He could directly create anything wicked—such as evil angels.[13] Hence, God did not create Lucifer and the fallen angels (demons) in a state of wickedness.

Now, though all the angels were originally created in a state of holiness, Scripture seems to imply that they were subjected to a period of probation. Some of the angels kept their first estate (a state of holiness); others did not (*see* Jude 6 KJV). In other words, some angels remained holy and did not sin, while others—following Lucifer's lead—rebelled against God and fell into great sin.[14] (We will address this angelic rebellion in great detail in chapter 14.)

It is highly significant that all the angels originally enjoyed God's direct presence (Matthew 18:10; Revelation 12:7-9) and heaven's perfect environment (Mark 13:32). This made the rebellion of some all the more sinful.[15]

. . . . .

Once the angels were put to the test to remain loyal to God or to rebel with Lucifer, their decision seems to have been made permanent in its effect. As theologian Charles Ryrie puts it, "Those who successfully passed the probationary test will always stay in that original holy state. Those who failed are now confirmed in their evil, rebellious state."[16]

Related to this is the fact that good angels are called "elect" angels in 1 Timothy 5:21. They are not elect because they sinned and then were elected unto redemption (remember, they *never sinned* during the probationary period). Rather, they are elect because God intervened to *permanently confirm ("elect") them in their holiness* so there would be no possibility of future sin on their part. Louis Berkhof says "they evidently received, in addition to the grace with which all angels were endowed, and which was sufficient to enable them to retain their position, a *special grace of perseverance*, by which they were confirmed in their position."[17] Thus, good angels are now incapable of sinning. The lines have been drawn, and they are now *absolute*.

This is confirmed by the testimony of Scripture, which says the evil angels who rebelled against God are *nonredeemable*. "Those that followed Satan in his sin fell decisively and are permanently left in their evil state without recourse or even the possibility of redemption. They are irrevocably consigned to the lake of fire (Matthew 25:41)."[18] Theologian Henry Thiessen suggests that "because the angels are a company and not a race, they sinned *individually*, and not in some federal head of the race [as was true with humanity's fall in the person of Adam]. It may be that because of this, God made no provision of salvation for the fallen angels."[19] The evil angels are destined for eternal suffering.

Where Do the Holy Angels Live?

Do angels just live invisibly on earth? Is stellar space their home? Or is their home to be found in the highest heaven where God Himself dwells?

Though angels apparently have access to the entire universe, God's Word seems to affirm that angels dwell in heaven but are sent out on specific errands or assignments, as was true in the case of Gabriel in Daniel 9:21 (cf. Mark 13:32).[20] There are numerous passages in Scripture which speak of heaven—and not earth—as the primary home of angels. For example:

• Micaiah makes reference to "the LORD sitting on his throne with all the host of heaven standing on his right and on his left" (2 Chronicles 18:18). The "host of heaven" refers specifically to the angelic realm.

• Daniel 7:10 makes reference to "thousands upon thousands" of angels attending God in heaven, and "ten thousand times ten thousand" (100 million) angels standing before Him.

• Isaiah 6:1-6 pictures angels hovering around God's throne, proclaiming, "Holy, holy, holy is the LORD Almighty."

• Jesus speaks of angels "ascending and descending" to and from heaven in John 1:51.

• Hebrews 12:22 exhorts believers, "You have come to . . . the city of the living God. You have come to thousands upon thousands of angels in joyful assembly."

• John the apostle, author of the book of Revelation, said, "I looked and heard the voice of many angels, numbering thousands upon thousands, and ten thousand times ten thousand. They encircled the throne and the living creatures and the elders" (Revelation 5:11).

It appears, then, that the natural habitat of angels is in heaven in the very presence of God. When they have an assigned task to perform, they leave the realm of

. . . . .

heaven, complete their work on earth (or wherever God sends them), and then return to heaven.

This, of course, is not to discount the possibility that some angels have *prolonged* assignments on earth. It is clear from a number of Scripture passages that God has appointed certain angels to guard and protect believers during their earthly sojourns. And what these angels do on behalf of God's children is quite different from what we read about in many of today's bestselling books about angels, as we will soon see.

*An angel is a spiritual creature
without a body created by God
for the service of Christendom
and the church.*

—Martin Luther[1]

·5·

The Nature of Angels

In late 1993 *Time* magazine conducted a poll asking people what they thought about the nature of angels. The findings indicated that some 55 percent of the American public believed angels are higher spiritual beings created by God with special powers to act as His agents on earth; 15 percent said they are the spirits of people who have died; 18 percent said they are an important religious idea but are merely symbolic; 7 percent said they are figments of the imagination.[2]

In this case, the majority (55 percent) come closest to the biblical view. The other views mentioned are patently false from a scriptural perspective.

As we address what Scripture says about the nature of angels, we must first note that the term "angel" indicates not the *nature* of angels but the *function*. The word *angel* simply means "messenger." Angels are God's messengers or ambassadors.[3] Saint Augustine put it this way: "The name Angel refers to their office, not their nature. You ask the name of this nature, it is spirit; you ask its office, it is that of an Angel, which is a messenger."[4]

In this chapter we will examine what Scripture says about the nature of these messengers of God. We will begin by drawing an important distinction between angels and humans.

Were Angels Once People?

According to the *Time* poll, 15 percent of Americans believe angels are the spirits of departed human beings—an idea popularized by a number of Hollywood movies. As we noted in the previous chapter, however, Christ Himself created the angels—and He created them *as angels* (Colossians 1:16).

We see the distinction between humans and angels reflected in a number of biblical passages. For example, Psalm 8:5 indicates that man was made lower than the angels, but shall be made higher in the afterlife (in heaven). In Hebrews 12:22-23 the "thousands upon thousands of angels" are clearly distinguished from the "spirits of righteous men made perfect." First Corinthians 6:3 tells us that there is coming a time when believers (in the afterlife) will judge angels. As well, 1 Corinthians 13:1 draws a distinction between the "tongues" (languages) of human beings and angels.[5] Clearly, humans and angels are portrayed as different classes of beings in the Bible.

Now, of course, angels and humans do have some similarities. For example, both are created beings; both are finite and limited; both are dependent upon God for their continued existence and well-being; both are responsible and accountable to God for their actions (*see* John 16:11; 1 Corinthians 6:3; Hebrews 9:27).[6] But even with those similarities, in terms of nature, humans and angels are in different classes altogether.

. . . . .

Angels Are Personal Beings

Just as you and I are persons, so also are angels persons (*spirit* persons)—with all the attributes of personality. (Keep in mind that *persons* here means not "people" but simply "beings with a personal nature.") Scripture portrays angels as possessing the personal attributes of intelligence, emotions, and a moral will.

• *Intelligence:* Angels are said to possess great wisdom (2 Samuel 14:20) and discernment (2 Samuel 14:17), and they use their minds to look into matters (1 Peter 1:12).

• *Emotions:* Angels are in "joyful assembly" in the presence of God in heaven (Hebrews 12:22). Moreover, they "shouted for joy" at the creation (Job 38:7), and there is "rejoicing in heaven" whenever a sinner repents (Luke 15:7).

• *Moral will:* Angels give evidence of having a moral will in the many moral decisions they make. For example, in Revelation 22:8-9 we see an angel exercise his moral will by forbidding John to worship him and acknowledging that worship belongs only to God.

Beyond having the attributes of personality, personal actions are also ascribed to angels. For example, angels *love and rejoice* (Luke 15:10); they *desire* (1 Peter 1:12); they *contend* (Jude 9; Revelation 12:7); they *worship* (Hebrews 1:6); they *talk* (Luke 1:13); and they *come and go* (John 1:51).[7] Clearly, then, angels are persons. As persons, they are able to render personal and intelligent worship of God (Psalm 148:2). They are also held responsible for the quality of their service and their moral choices (*see* 1 Corinthians 6:3).[8] And, it is as persons that God sends angels as ministering spirits (Hebrews 1:14), bringing aid and protection to His people.

. . . . .

Angels Are Incorporeal and Invisible

The Scriptures tell us that angels are incorporeal and invisible. The word *incorporeal* means "lacking material form or substance." Angels, then, are not material, physical beings; they are spirit beings and are hence invisible. (This doesn't contradict the idea that angels can *appear* to humans; more on this later.)

It is interesting to note that some Jews and early church fathers believed that angels have some kind of airy or fiery bodies. They found it difficult to understand how a true creature could lack a body.[9] Theologians later concluded that angels are pure spirit beings. They based this view on passages like Hebrews 1:14, where angels are called "ministering spirits."

Because angels do not have physical bodies, they know nothing of what it is like to get ill, grow old, decay, and eventually die.[10] Angels know nothing of the limitations that are part and parcel of having a physical body.[11] God created them as *nonphysical* beings.

In addition, because angels are invisible, you and I are generally unaware of their activities behind the scenes. There is no telling just how many times angels have intervened on our behalf without our being aware of it.

We will soon see that angels, even though they are by nature invisible and incorporeal, have the ability to appear visibly to human beings. But normally, angels are not visible to the human eye. You may recall from the Old Testament that the Lord had to "open" Balaam's eyes before he could see that an angel was standing in his way (Numbers 22:31). The prophet Elisha had to ask the Lord to "open" the eyes of his servant; *then* the young man was able to see a multitude of angelic beings on the mountainside, protecting him and Elisha from their enemies (2 Kings 6:17).

. . . . .

Billy Graham has some great insights on man's inability to see angels. Consider his words:

> While angels may become visible by choice, our eyes are not constructed to see them ordinarily any more than we can see the dimensions of a nuclear field, the structure of atoms, or the electricity that flows through copper wiring. Our ability to sense reality is limited: The deer of the forest far surpass our human capacity in their keenness of smell. Bats possess a phenomenally sensitive built-in radar system. Some animals can see things in the dark that escape our attention. Swallows and geese possess sophisticated guidance systems that appear to border on the supernatural. So why should we think it strange if men fail to perceive the evidences of angelic presence?[12]

All things considered, it may be that one reason God chose to keep humans from being able to perceive angels is man's tendency to worship and venerate the creation in place of the Creator.[13] Remember what happened to the apostle John? When he was receiving the "revelation" from the Lord and beheld a mighty angel, his first inclination was to bow down and worship the angel. But the angel instructed John to cease and to render worship *only to God* (Revelation 22:8-9). Perhaps as a safeguard, then, God purposefully designed man with the inability to perceive His glorious angels.

Angels Are Localized

Even though angels are spirit beings, they seem to have spatial limitations. They cannot be everywhere at once; Scripture clearly portrays them as having to move from one place to another.

An example of this would be when the angel Gabriel engaged in "swift flight" to travel from heaven to Daniel's side (Daniel 9:21-23). Then, in Daniel 10:10-14, we read about a different angel who was delayed on his errand by another spirit being—apparently a demon. One Bible scholar made this observation about the delay: "Here a time limitation corresponds with spatial limitation. If a time lapse is involved in their changing locations, this means they are localized."[14]

After a group of angels appeared visibly to some shepherds in a field to announce the birth of Christ, the angels "left them" and went back "into heaven" (Luke 2:15). Angels can only be in one place at a time and must engage in spatial travel to go from one place to another. Even Christ Himself spoke of angels "ascending and descending" from heaven (John 1:51).

Do All Angels Have Wings?

Angels are commonly depicted on postcards, cartoons, magazines, and other literature as having wings. But do *all* angels have wings?

Scripture makes it clear to us that *many* angels have wings. For example, the seraphim described in Isaiah 6:1-5 have wings. The cherubim Ezekiel saw in his vision have wings (Ezekiel 1:6). The angels the apostle John saw in his vision have wings (Revelation 4:8). But there are many other Bible verses about angels that make no mention of wings (for example, Hebrews 13:2). What can we conclude from this?

Though it is possible that all of God's angels have wings, this is not a necessary inference. Theologian Millard Erickson explains that "the cherubim and seraphim are represented as winged (Exodus 25:20;

Isaiah 6:2) . . . . However, we have no assurance that what is true of cherubim and seraphim is true of angels in general. Since there is no explicit reference indicating that angels *as a whole* are winged, we must regard this as at best an inference, but not a necessary inference, from the biblical passages which describe them as flying."[15]

Some people have suggested that the wings of angels are symbolic and may not actually be necessary for flight. "The wings pictured in angelic visions (note they do not always appear with wings) may be symbols of their swiftness to execute God's wishes, just as wind and fire symbolize their fast and fervent service (Hebrews 1:7)."[16]

It is also important to recognize that for angels to have wings does not contradict what we learned earlier about angels as spirit beings who are by nature invisible and incorporeal (Hebrews 1:14). Winged angels are spirit beings who are nonphysical and are naturally invisible to the human eye.

Angels Can Appear as Men

Though angels are normally invisible, they *can* nevertheless appear as men (Matthew 1:20; Luke 1:26; John 20:12).[17] Their resemblance to men can be so realistic, in fact, that they are actually taken to *be* human beings (Hebrews 13:2).

Recall from the Old Testament that Abraham welcomed three "men" in the plains of Mamre (Genesis 18:1-8). These "men" walked, talked, sat down, and ate—just like normal men—but they *were not* men; they were angels (*see* Genesis 18:22; 19:1).[18] Now, we have no scriptural evidence that angels need food for sustenance.[19] But apparently they can appear as men and *eat* like men during the course of fulfilling their assigned task in the realm of humanity.

. . . . .

Thus, it is altogether possible that a particular person who helped you during a time of need in your past was actually an angel who *appeared* as a human. There is no reason to suggest that such appearances cannot occur today just as they did in biblical times.

Angels Are Powerful

The Scriptures portray angels as extremely powerful and mighty beings. Indeed, Psalm 103:20 calls them "mighty ones who do his bidding." Second Thessalonians 1:7 makes reference to God's "powerful angels."

An example of angelic strength may be found in Matthew 28, where we read that an angel rolled away the giant stone at the sepulcher of Jesus (verses 2-7). Some people have estimated that a wheel of granite much like the one that guarded the tomb—about eight feet in diameter and one foot thick—would weigh over four tons (8,000 pounds).[20] Yet an angel flipped the stone out of the way as if it were a mere pebble.

It seems from Scripture that some angels are more powerful than others. As noted earlier, Daniel 10:13 tells us that an angel who had been sent by God to accomplish a task was detained by a more powerful fallen angel (a demon). It was only when the archangel Michael showed up to render aid that the lesser angel was freed to carry out his task.

Angels Are Not Omnipotent

Even though angels are great in power, we must also emphasize that none of them (including the archangel Michael) are omnipotent (all-powerful) like God is. Angels are creatures with creaturely limitations.

This is important to observe because *angels are no replacement for God*—as some New Age angel enthusiasts imply in their writings. The power of angels is derived from and dependent upon God. And their power is always exercised on behalf of God, never toward achieving their own ends.

Angels Are Holy

We noted in the previous chapter that those angels who passed their probationary test and did not sin were confirmed in their holiness (*see* 1 Timothy 5:21). But what does it mean to be holy?

The word *holy* comes from a root word that means "set apart." God's angels are set apart from sin and set apart unto God to serve Him and carry out His assigned tasks.

It is interesting to note that many times in Scripture the angels are simply referred to as God's "holy ones" (Job 5:1; 15:15; Psalm 89:7; Daniel 4:13,17,23; 8:13; Jude 14). They are set apart unto God in every way. Their commitment to Him is complete. Their joy is found in pleasing their Creator.

All this is in marked contrast to the fallen angels— demons—who are *un*holy in every way. *They* are set apart from righteousness and set apart unto the Devil to do his unholy bidding. They are against everything related to God. As we will see later on, however, their time is limited, and their ultimate destiny is the lake of fire.

Angels Are Obedient

Related to the description of angels as God's "holy ones" is the fact that angels are obedient to God. Their holiness is reflected in their obedience to their Creator. In Psalm 103:20, the psalmist exults, "Praise the LORD, you his angels, you mighty ones who *do his bidding*, who *obey his word*" (emphasis added).

As we noted earlier, angels do not interact among humans to do their own bidding. Rather, they act under instruction from God. The only reason angels minister to believers during their earthly sojourns is because God has ordained it to be so.

Another verse that speaks of the obedience of God's holy angels is Matthew 6:10. In this part of the Lord's Prayer we find the words, "Your kingdom come, your will be done on earth as it is in heaven." On the surface, this may seem an unlikely verse in support of the obedience of angels. But many scholars believe Matthew 6:10 is saying, "May God's will be done among humans on earth as it is already being done by the holy angels in heaven." If this interpretation is correct, then the angels set an example for us in what it means to be obedient to God without wavering.

Angels Have Great Knowledge

Though angels are not omniscient (all-knowing) like God is, they do possess great wisdom and intelligence. One indication of this is that angels were created as a higher order of creatures in the universe than humans (*see* Psalm 8:5). Therefore, they innately possess a greater knowledge than man.

Beyond this, angels gain ever-increasing knowledge through long observation of human activities. Unlike people, angels do not have to study the past; they have *experienced* it. They have witnessed firsthand how other people have acted and reacted in certain situations and thus can predict with a great degree of accuracy how we may act in similar circumstances. The experiences of longevity give angels greater knowledge.[21]

. . . . .

Angels Are Immortal

Angels live forever. Once created, they never cease to exist. Indeed, Scripture clearly states that angels are not subject to death (Luke 20:36).[22]

It is interesting to note that in Daniel 9 the angel Gabriel appeared to the prophet Daniel. Then, more than 500 years later, this *same* unaged Gabriel appeared to Zechariah, the father of John the Baptist (Luke 1).[23]

Since angels are immortal and do not die—and since they do not propagate baby angels (Matthew 22:30)—it appears that the number of angels is and always will be the same.[24] The number of angelic beings that presently exist is identical to the number originally created by God.

Bringing the Facts Together

In our brief survey we have discovered a number of fascinating insights about the nature of angels:

• Angels are not departed human beings. When angels were created by God, they were created *as angels*.

• Angels are *personal beings* with all the attributes of personality—mind, emotions, and will.

• Angels are *incorporeal* (lacking material substance) and *invisible*.

• Though angels are invisible, they have the *ability to appear* to humans.

• Angels are *localized* and have to engage in spatial travel to go from one place to another.

• Some (possibly even all) angels *have wings*.

• Angels have *great power*, though they are not omnipotent (all-powerful).

• Angels are *holy* (they are set apart from sin and set apart unto God).

. . . . .

• Angels are *obedient* to God.

• Angels possess *greater intelligence* than humans though they are not omniscient (all-knowing) like God.

• Angels are *immortal* and do not die.

And that is just the beginning of what the Bible tells us about angels!

*That the universe should be ordered
around a series of over/under
hierarchical relationships is God's idea,
a part of His original design.*

—Duane Litfin[1]

·6·

The Organization of Angels

There has been much speculation regarding just how many angels there are. The great logician Thomas Aquinas believed there are many times more angels than there are human beings.[2] Saint Albert the Great calculated that there were exactly 399,920,004 angels.[3] The Kabbalists of medieval Judaism determined there were precisely 301,655,722 angels.[4]

Clement of Alexandria in the second century A.D. suggested that there are as many angels as there are stars in the stellar heavens.[5] This line of thinking is based on the idea that angels are associated with the stars in Scripture (Job 38:7; Psalm 148:1-3; Revelation 9:1-2; 12:3-4,7-9). If Clement is correct, the number of angels would exceed the stars visible to the human eye—approximately 6,000 during a year. Scientists say the total number of stars in the universe may run into the billions.[6]

The Scriptures use terminology indicating that the number of angels is vast indeed. We find reference to "a great company of the heavenly host" (Luke 2:13), and the angels are spoken of as "tens of thousands and thousands of thousands" (Psalm 68:17; cf. Daniel 7:10). Their number is elsewhere described as "myriads of myriads" (Revelation 5:11 NASB).

Daniel 7:10, speaking of God, says that "thousands upon thousands [of angels] attended him; ten thousand times ten thousand stood before him." The number "ten thousand times ten thousand" is 100,000,000 (100 million). This is a number almost too vast to fathom. Job 25:3 understandably asks, "Can his forces be numbered?"

Theologian Charles Ryrie says "some have suggested that there are as many angels in the universe as the total number of all human beings throughout history."[7] He further suggests this may be implied in the words of Jesus recorded in Matthew 18:10: "See that you do not look down on one of these little ones. For I tell you that their angels in heaven always see the face of my Father in heaven." Some people reason that this could be interpreted to mean that every child who has ever lived has had an angelic counterpart in heaven.

Scripture never specifies for us just how many angels there are. But one thing is certain: However many angels there are, there is certainly no increase or decrease in their number. We have noted earlier that angels do not die, nor do they propagate and give birth to baby angels. The number of angels remains perfectly constant at all times.[8]

Ranks in the Angelic Realm

Not only are the angels of God numerous, but they are also well organized. Our God is a God of order, and this characteristic is reflected in the angelic realm. There are angels of different ranks and power, and these angels individually and collectively serve God in the outworking of His sovereign will. Let's note what Scripture says about their varying ranks:

• In Colossians 1:16 we read, "By [Christ] all things were created: things in heaven and on earth, visible and invisible, whether *thrones* or *powers* or *rulers* or *authorities*; all things were created by him and for him"[9] (emphasis added).

• Colossians 2:10 says Christ "is the head over every *power* and *authority*."

• In 1 Peter 3:22 we read that Christ "has gone into heaven and is at God's right hand—with *angels, authorities* and *powers* in submission to him" (emphasis added).

• Ephesians 1:20-21 speaks of Christ's authority as being "far above all *rule* and *authority, power* and *dominion*, and every title that can be given, not only in the present age but also in the one to come" (emphasis added).

What do the terms *rulers, principalities, powers, thrones*, and *dominions* mean in these and other such verses? In the rabbinic (Jewish) thought of the first century, these words were used to describe the hierarchical organization in the angelic realm. Reformed scholar Louis Berkhof says, "These appellations do not point to different kinds of angels, but simply to differences of rank or dignity among them."[10]

It is difficult to say for sure what the specific terms mean in reference to the various ranks of angels. But theologians have suggested some likely interpretations.

It may be that the angels known as *thrones* are angelic beings whose place is in the immediate presence of God—in the immediate vicinity of His glorious throne.[11] It is possible that they even sit on their own lesser thrones, pointing to their derived authority under the greater authority of God.[12] These beings may be invested with regal power by which they carry out the sovereign bidding of God. Clement of Alexandria, an early church father, offered an alternate view, suggesting that *thrones* were so called because they either formed or supported the throne of Almighty God.[13]

The *dominions* are apparently next in dignity to the angels known as *thrones*.[14] These angels exercise dominion over specific *domains* in carrying out the sovereign bidding of God.

The angels called *rulers* are next in line and exercise rule as assigned by God. We are not told what their rule consists of. But like the other angels in authority, the "ruler angels" reflect the fact that God is characterized by order and organization in the way He governs the universe.

The angels known as *authorities* are possibly subordinate authorities who serve under one of the other orders of angels.[15] Again, we are not told any specifics, but these angelic beings clearly carry out imperial responsibility.[16]

Renowned Bible expositor Joseph Lightfoot makes the important point that the combination of the words *rulers* and *authorities* are applied "not only to good angels but to bad, not only to spiritual powers but to earthly."[17] Just as there are humans in authority over other humans, so also are there holy angels in authority over other holy angels, and fallen angels in authority over other fallen angels.

Beyond these specific angelic ranks, Scripture also speaks of other angels who have varying levels of authority and dignity—including the archangel Michael, the cherubim, the seraphim, and Gabriel. Let us briefly consider each of these.

. . . . .

Michael the Archangel

The word *archangel* implies a rank first among angels. Apparently Michael is in authority over all the other angels—including the thrones, dominions, rulers, and authorities. The term *archangel* occurs just twice in the New Testament, and in both instances it is used in the singular and is preceded by the definite article *the* ("the archangel"—1 Thessalonians 4:16; Jude 9). Some scholars conclude from this that the term is restricted to a single archangel—Michael.[18]

Charles Ryrie, for example, says, "Only Michael is designated as the archangel or high-ranking angel (Jude 9; 1 Thessalonians 4:16). Nowhere does the Bible speak of archangels, though there evidently are other high-ranking angels (Daniel 10:13), yet only one archangel. When Paul says that the voice of the archangel will be heard at the [Rapture] of the church, he does not seem to feel the need to name that archangel, which supports the conclusion that there is only one."[19]

Other scholars, however, say that "the definite article ['the'] with archangel does not necessarily limit the class of archangel to Michael. The article may be one of identification as the *well-known* archangel instead of limitation as the *only* archangel. There may be others of the same class or rank, since he is described as 'one of the chief princes' (Daniel 10:13)."[20] Jewish tradition has always held that there are seven archangels.[21]

Regardless of whether there is one or more than one archangel, Michael is undeniably the prominent archangel. He is called a chief prince (Daniel 10:13) and "the great prince" (Daniel 12:1), and the other angels seem to be led by him (Revelation 12:7). Bible scholar Clinton Arnold tells us that the word "prince" is a title of authority and, when used of angels, refers to beings in authority over a host of angels in battle. Michael, as a *chief* prince and *great* prince (and *especially* as the archangel) would be in authority over all the "prince angels."[22]

Michael appears to be specially related to Israel as her guardian (Daniel 12:1). Louis Berkhof says of Michael, "We see in him the valiant warrior fighting the battles of Jehovah against the enemies of Israel and against the evil powers in the spirit-world."[23]

Michael's name means "Who is like God?"[24] His name humbly points to the incomparability of God. It speaks of Michael's complete and unwavering devotedness to God, which stands in stark contrast with Satan, who in his pride declared, "I will be like the most High" (Isaiah 14:14 KJV).[25]

Now, a controversial question that comes up from time to time relates to the claim that appearances of Michael in the Bible were actually appearances of Jesus Christ, the second person of the triune Godhead. Is this a possibility, or does Scripture forbid such an interpretation? I believe there are at least five biblical arguments that make such an interpretation impossible. Let us briefly consider these arguments.

1. *The archangel Michael does not have the authority in himself to rebuke Satan.* Jude 9 tells us, "But Michael the archangel, when he disputed with the devil and argued about the body of Moses, did not dare pronounce against him a railing judgment, but said, 'The Lord rebuke you'" (NASB). By contrast, Jesus rebuked the Devil on a number of different occasions (*see,* for example, Matthew 4:10 and 16:23). Since Michael *could not* rebuke the Devil in his own authority and Jesus *could* (and *did*) rebuke the Devil in His own authority, Michael and Jesus cannot be the same person.

Notice that Michael the Archangel said, "the *Lord* rebuke you." The Greek word for "Lord" in this verse is *kurios*. It is the standard word for "Lord" in the New

Testament. It is also a direct parallel to the word *Yahweh* or *Jehovah* in the Old Testament. It is highly significant that Jesus is called *kurios* ("Lord") many times in the New Testament (as opposed to Michael, who is never called *kurios*).

For example, we are told that Jesus is *kurios* ("Lord") in Philippians 2:9-11, and that at the name of Jesus every knee will bow in heaven and on earth and under the earth, and every tongue will confess that *Jesus is Lord*. The apostle Paul, an Old Testament scholar par excellence, is here alluding to Isaiah 45:22-24: "I am God, and there is no other. By myself I have sworn, my mouth has uttered in all integrity a word that will not be revoked: Before me every knee will bow; by me every tongue will swear." Paul was drawing on his vast knowledge of the Old Testament to make the point that Jesus Christ is *kurios* and *Yahweh*—the *Lord* of all humankind.

Now, the point of my saying all this is that when Michael said, "The *Lord* rebuke you," he was appealing directly to the sovereign authority of the Lord of the universe. And *Jesus is clearly the sovereign Lord of the universe*.

2. *In Daniel 10:13 Michael is called "one of the chief princes."* Whether or not there is more than one archangel, the fact that Michael is "one of" the chief princes indicates that he is *one among a group* of chief princes. How large that group is, we are not told. But the scriptural statement that Michael is one in a group proves that he is not utterly unique. By contrast, the Greek word used to describe Jesus in John 3:16 is *monogenēs*—which means "unique," "one of a kind."

Jesus is never called "chief prince" in the Bible. In fact, He is called the "King of kings and Lord of lords" in Revelation 19:16. This is a title that indicates absolute sovereignty and authority. A King of kings/Lord of lords is much higher in authority than a mere "chief prince" (who is one in a group of princes). The former has absolute sovereignty and authority; the latter has derived, limited authority.

3. *Hebrews 1:5 tells us that no angel can ever be called God's son.* Since Jesus *is* the Son of God, and since no angel can ever be called God's son, then Jesus cannot possibly be the archangel Michael.

4. *Hebrews 1:6 tells us that Christ is worshiped by the angels.* This is the exact same word (Greek: *proskuneo*) used of worshiping Jehovah God in the Bible. Christ is worshiped with the same kind of worship rendered to the Father (cf. Revelation 4:10-11; 5:11-12). There is no getting around this fact. Jesus is not an angel; He is *worshiped* by the angels.

Commentator Ray Stedman notes that in the Old Testament, "the angels are called to worship Yahweh (Jehovah). New Testament writers apply such passages without hesitation to Jesus. Many places in Scripture witness the obedience of the angels, notably Job 38:7, Luke 2:13, and Revelation 5:11-12. Mark 3:11 indicates that even the demons (fallen angels) fell down before Jesus when they saw him and addressed him as the Son of God."[26]

5. *We are explicitly told in Hebrews 2:5 that the world is not (and never will be) in subjection to an angel.* Certain angels—such as the archangel Michael, principalities, powers, dominions, and thrones—have various ranks and, under God, exercise imperial authority in different ways. But *no* angel is ever said to rule the world or God's kingdom.

The backdrop to Hebrews 2:5 is that the Dead Sea Scrolls (discovered at Qumran in 1947) reflect an expectation that the archangel Michael would be a supreme figure in the coming messianic kingdom. It may be that some of the recipients of the book of Hebrews were tempted to assign angels a place above Christ. Whether or not this is so, Hebrews 2:5 makes it absolutely clear that *no* angel (Michael included) will rule God's kingdom.

If no angel can rule the world (Hebrews 2:5), then *Christ cannot be the archangel Michael* since Christ is said to be the Ruler of God's kingdom over and over again in Scripture (for example, Genesis 49:10; 2 Samuel 7:16; Psalm 2:6; Daniel 7:13-14; Matthew 2:1-2; Luke 1:32-33; Revelation 19:16).

Now, all of this is pointed out not to denigrate Michael in any way but rather to draw the very important distinction between Christ as eternal Creator-God and Michael the created archangel. Michael is a creature with creaturely limitations. And he exists to carry out Christ's sovereign bidding.

The Cherubim:
Angels of Power and Majesty

The cherubim are depicted in Scripture as powerful and majestic angelic creatures who surround God's throne and defend His holiness from any contamination by sin (Genesis 3:24; Exodus 25:18,20; Ezekiel 1:1-18).[27] They are portrayed as being indescribably beautiful and powerful spirit-beings of the highest order (Ezekiel 1:5-14; 28:12-14,17).

Ezekiel 1 speaks of four living creatures in the midst of a burning fire. Later on, they are explicitly identified as cherubim (Ezekiel 10:1). Expositor Charles Dyer summarizes Ezekiel's description of the cherubim this way:

> The general appearance of the living beings was somewhat like a man. However, they would not be mistaken for humans.

They each had four faces and four wings. . . .
The cherubim's legs were straight, which
implies that they were standing upright, but
their feet were calf-like instead of human,
and were like burnished (highly polished)
bronze. Ezekiel said the four cherubim also
had human-like hands . . . .Having four faces
on four sides of their heads and being con-
nected in a square, they were able to travel
straight in any direction and to change
direction without turning.[28]

The cherubim—obviously very high-ranking angels—
are pictured as guarding Eden after the expulsion of
Adam and Eve (Genesis 3:24). Figures of cherubim
adorned the ark and were positioned in such a way that
they gazed upon the mercy seat (Exodus 25:17-20). Cherubim also adorned Solomon's Temple (1 Kings 6:23-35).
They were represented on the veil which barred the
entrance to the Holy of Holies.[29] As well, cherubim are
portrayed in the Old Testament as the chariot on which
God descends to the earth (2 Samuel 22:11; Psalm 18:10).

The etymology of the word *cherubim* is not known
for certain, though some have suggested that the word
means "to guard." Certainly this meaning would fit well
with their function of guarding the entrance of Eden
(Genesis 3:24). This meaning also fits with the cherubim
on the Temple veil that barred entrance into the Holy of
Holies (Exodus 26:31; 2 Chronicles 3:14). Here, the cherubim are apparently guardians of the holiness of God.

It is interesting to note that even though the cherubim are portrayed as angels in Scripture, they are never
actually *called* angels. This may be because they do not
function as messengers in their duties. (Remember, the
word *angel* literally means "messenger.") The cherubim

are never seen bringing revelation or instruction from God to men.[30]

The Seraphim: God's "Burning Ones"

We encounter angels known as seraphim only in Isaiah's vision recorded in Isaiah 6. Consider Isaiah's words:

> In the year that King Uzziah died, I saw the Lord seated on a throne, high and exalted, and the train of his robe filled the temple.
>
> Above him were seraphs, each with six wings: With two wings they covered their faces, with two they covered their feet, and with two they were flying.
>
> And they were calling to one another: "Holy, holy, holy is the LORD Almighty; the whole earth is full of his glory."
>
> At the sound of their voices the doorposts and thresholds shook and the temple was filled with smoke.
>
> "Woe to me!" I cried. "I am ruined! For I am a man of unclean lips, and I live among a people of unclean lips, and my eyes have seen the King, the LORD Almighty."
>
> Then one of the seraphs flew to me with a live coal in his hand, which he had taken with tongs from the altar.
>
> With it he touched my mouth and said, "See, this has touched your lips; your guilt is taken away and your sin atoned for" (Isaiah 6:1-7).

It is highly revealing that the Hebrew term for *seraphim* literally means "burning ones."[31] This no doubt speaks of their consuming devotion to serving God. "They are afire with adoration of the holy God. Their great cry is in praise of the perfect holiness of God. To ascribe the term 'holy' to God three times means, according to Hebrew idiom, to recognize God as extremely, perfectly holy. Therefore, they *praise and proclaim the perfect holiness of God*."[32]

It has been suggested that the wings of the seraphim are loaded with symbolic meaning: The fact that two wings cover their faces seems to communicate that even the holy angels cannot look upon the full, unveiled glory of God. (First Timothy 6:16 tells us that God dwells in "unapproachable light.") That two wings cover their feet apparently symbolizes their reverence (perhaps this points to their hesitancy in treading on "holy ground"). With their third pair of wings the seraphim fly—swiftly carrying out commands they receive from God on the throne.[33]

Gabriel: Mighty One of God

The name *Gabriel* literally means "mighty one of God." The name speaks of Gabriel's incredible power as endowed by God. He is distinguished as an angel who stands in the very presence of God (Luke 1:19), evidently in some preeminent sense.[34] His high rank in the angelic realm is obvious from both his name and his continuous standing in the presence of God. When carrying out the bidding of God, Gabriel apparently has the ability to fly swiftly—perhaps faster than most of the other angels (Daniel 9:21).

Gabriel is portrayed in Scripture as one who brings revelation to the people of God regarding God's purpose and program.[35] For example, in the Old Testament he appeared to the prophet Daniel (Daniel 8:16; 9:21). Gabriel revealed the future by interpreting a vision for

. . . . .

Daniel (8:17), and gave understanding and wisdom to him (9:22).[36] In the New Testament (some 500 years later), Gabriel brought the message to Zechariah about the birth of John the Baptist, and announced the birth of Jesus to the Virgin Mary (Luke 1:11-17,26-38).[37]

Some people may be tempted to think that Gabriel's responsibility of bringing revelation to human beings is a lowly one unbefitting to one of heaven's greatest angels. This is not the case, however. The fact is, out of all the angels in the universe, God entrusted *to Gabriel alone* the greatest messages that *ever left the courts of heaven*—including the message of Christ's approaching birth. In choosing Gabriel for such tasks, God honored the great angel before the entire angelic realm.[38]

God's Ordered Universe

The biblical worldview is based on the assumption that a personal God sovereignly designed an ordered universe to function in a particular way. Crucial to this worldview is the concept of authority. Romans 13:1 tells us that God is the source not simply of all authority but of the very *concept* of authority. "That the universe should be ordered around a series of over/under hierarchical relationships is His idea, a part of His original design. He delegates His authority according to His own pleasure to those whom He places in appropriate positions and it is to Him that His creatures submit when they acknowledge that authority."[39]

God has set up an authority structure within the church (1 Timothy 2:11-15; 1 Corinthians 11:2-16; 14:33-36). He has set up an authority structure within the family unit (1 Corinthians 11:3; Ephesians 5:22-23). He has likewise set up an authority structure in the angelic realm (Ephesians 1:20-21; Colossians 1:16; 2:10; 1 Peter 3:22).

And all of these lesser authorities are in submission to the greater authority of Christ Himself (Colossians 2:10).

As Christians, we should take great comfort in how God has set up His universe. For He has ordained various authority structures—including that of the entire angelic realm—for the optimum benefit of His creatures and for the outworking of His sovereign will in the universe.

For the ancients a name is not simply
a conventional designation,
but rather an expression of a being's
place in the universe.

—Henri Cazelles[1]

·7·

Titles of Angels

In the ancient world a name or title was not a mere label as it is today. Rather, a name or title was considered a statement that revealed something about the person bearing it. We learn something of the nature and function of a person by studying his or her name or title.

As we read the Scriptures, it becomes clear that the various titles ascribed to angels reveal a great deal about them. In the Bible we find that angels are called sons of God, ministering spirits, God's heavenly host, holy ones, and watchers, among various other titles. Let's examine these representative titles with a view to learning more about the nature and function of angels.

Angels As Sons of God

Earlier we noted that in a number of places in the Bible, angels are referred to as "sons of God" (for example, Job 1:6; 2:1; 38:7 KJV). What does this title mean in reference to angels? And how does it differ from the designation "Son of God" as used of Jesus Christ?

It is essential to recognize that the words "son of..." can carry different meanings in different contexts. A look at any Greek lexicon makes this abundantly clear. Hence, the term can be used in one way in regard to angels and quite another way when used of the person of Jesus Christ.

Theologians are vitually unanimous in saying that angels are sons of God in the sense of being *created directly by the hand of God.*[2] The phrase "sons of God," when used of angels, simply denotes spirit-beings who were brought into existence by a direct creative act of God.[3] Every angel that exists was a direct creation of God.

Remember also that angels do not give birth to other angels (Matthew 22:30). Hence, we never read of "sons of angels." Since every single angel was *directly* created by the hand of God, it is appropriate that they be called "sons of God."

If the phrase "sons of God" in Genesis 6:2-4 is a reference to fallen angels, as many Bible expositors believe, then even fallen angels are called "sons of God" in the sense that they were created by God. Of course, they were not *created* as fallen angels. These particular angels rebelled against God some time after their creation and *became* fallen.

Now, how does all this relate to Christ being called the "Son of God"? This is an important question, for Christ is not in the same league as the angels (though some cultists try to argue that He is). A person will go far astray unless he or she sees a clear distinction between Christ as the *Son of God* and angels as *sons of God.* As we will see, the Bible indicates that Christ is *eternally* the Son of God. How do we know this? Consider the following.

To begin, a word study of the term "son of..." indicates that it can mean "of the order of" in certain contexts.[4] The phrase is often used this way in the Old Testament. For example, "sons of the prophets" meant "of the order of prophets" (1 Kings 20:35). "Sons of the singers" meant "of the order of singers" (Nehemiah 12:28 KJV). Likewise, the phrase "Son of God," used of Christ, means "of the order of God" and represents a claim to undiminished deity.

Ancient Semites and Orientals sometimes used the phrase "son of . . ." to indicate likeness or sameness of nature and equality of being.[5] When Jesus claimed to be the Son of God, His Jewish contemporaries fully understood that He was using the term in this way—making a claim to be God in an unqualified sense. Benjamin Warfield affirms that, from the earliest days of Christianity, the phrase "Son of God"—when used of Jesus Christ—was understood to be fully equivalent to God.[6]

This is why, when Jesus claimed to be the Son of God, the Jews tried to kill Him: "For this reason the Jews tried all the harder to kill him; not only was he breaking the Sabbath, but he was even calling God his own Father, making himself equal with God" (John 5:18). The Jews later said, "We have a law, and according to that law he [Christ] must die, because he claimed to be the Son of God" (John 19:7, insert added). The Jews recognized that Jesus was identifying Himself as God and wanted to put Him to death for what they thought was blasphemy (*see* Leviticus 24:16).

Clear evidence for Christ's eternal sonship is found in God's Word; He is represented as *already being* the Son of God before His human birth in Bethlehem. Recall Jesus' discussion with Nicodemus in John 3, for instance, when He said, "God so loved the world that he *gave* his one and only Son, that whoever believes in him shall not perish but have eternal life. For God did not *send* his Son *into* the world to condemn the world, but to save the world through him" (John 3:16-17, emphasis added). That Christ, *as the Son of God*, was *sent into* the world implies that He was the Son *before* the incarnation.

Related to this, chapter 30 in the book of Proverbs was authored by a godly man named Agur. In the first four verses, Agur reflects on man's inability to comprehend the infinite God. Because of this inability, he abases himself and humbly acknowledges his ignorance. He effectively communicates the idea that reverence of God is the beginning of true wisdom.

In verse 4, Agur's reflections are couched in a series of questions. He asks:

> Who has gone up to heaven and come down? Who has gathered up the wind in the hollow of his hands?
> Who has wrapped up the waters in his cloak? Who has established all the ends of the earth?
> What is his name, and the name of his son? Tell me if you know!"

Many scholars—including renowned Old Testament scholars F. Delitzsch and A.R. Fausset—concede that this verse is likely an Old Testament reference to the first and second persons of the Trinity, the eternal Father and the eternal Son of God.[7] And it is highly significant that this portion of Scripture is not predictive prophecy—it is not speaking about a *future* Son of God. Rather, it speaks of God the Father and God the Son in *present-tense terms* during *Old Testament times*.

Obviously, the answer to each of the four questions in Proverbs 30:4 must be *God*. And the very fact that Agur asked about the name of God's Son seems to imply a recognition, by divine inspiration, of plurality within the Godhead.[8]

. . . . .

We find further evidence for Christ's eternal son-
ship in Hebrews 1:2, which says God created the uni-
verse *through* his "Son"—implying that Christ was the
Son of God *prior* to the Creation. Moreover, Christ *as the
Son* is explicitly said to have existed "before all things"
(Colossians 1:17; compare with verses 13-14). As well,
Jesus, speaking as the Son of God (John 8:54-56), asserts
His eternal preexistence before Abraham (verse 58).

Clearly, then, Scripture affirms that Jesus is *eternally*
the Son of God. Any attempt to relegate Christ to a
position *less* than God simply because of His title "Son of
God" is to woefully misunderstand what the term really
meant among the ancients.

In contrast, angels as "sons of God" are *created
beings;* in fact, Scripture tells us that the angels were
created by Jesus Christ, the Son of God (Colossians 1:16;
cf. John 1:3; Hebrews 1:2,10). This in itself sets a wide
chasm between Christ and the angels. After all, the same
Bible that tells us *Christ* created the angels also tells us
that *only God* can be the Creator (Isaiah 44:24).

Angels As Ministering Spirits

Hebrews 1:14 asks, "Are not all angels ministering
spirits sent to serve those who will inherit salvation?"
This brief statement about angels is packed with meaning.

The word "ministering" comes from a Greek word
that means "to serve." Angels are *spirit-servants* who
render aid to believers in the outworking of God's purpose on earth. And notice that the author of Hebrews
says *"all* angels" fall into this category. "Even the most
exalted angel is employed in the comparatively humble
office of a ministering spirit appointed to assist the heirs
of salvation."[9]

What form does this service take? Popular author Ray Stedman says "such ministry involves protection (Psalm 91:11), guidance (Genesis 19:16-17), encouragement (Judges 6:12), deliverance (Acts 12:7), supply (Psalm 105:40), enlightenment (Matthew 2:19-20), and empowerment (Luke 22:43)."[10] Stedman also notes that "their service is rendered largely unseen and often unrecognized, but a passage like [Hebrews 1:14] should make us watchful for such help and grateful to the gracious Lord who sends angels to our aid."[11]

Notice that Hebrews 1:14 tells us that angels are *sent* to render service to the heirs of salvation. The angels are specifically appointed by God to carry out tasks on behalf of believers. They are all under His control, and are in a subordinate position to Him. It is important to keep this in mind, for many angel enthusiasts today have focused so much attention on angels that God is left entirely out of the picture. We must never forget that angels assist us because *God has ordained it that way*.

Commenting on Hebrews 1:14, expositor Albert Barnes says that "it is a great principle of the divine administration that one class of God's creatures are to minister to others; that one is to aid another—to assist him in trouble, to provide for him when poor, and to counsel him in perplexity."[12] Barnes keenly points out, "As man was ruined in the fall by the temptation offered by one of an angelic, though fallen nature [Satan], why should not others of angelic, unfallen holiness come to assist in repairing the evils which their fallen, guilty brethren have inflicted on the race?"[13]

Within God's sovereign plan, then, the angels assist human beings. This amounts to the strong aiding the weak, the enlightened aiding the ignorant, the pure aiding the impure, and the unfallen aiding the fallen. And this assistance often comes when we're not even aware of it. "So it may be a part of the great arrangements of divine Providence that many of the most needed and acceptable interpositions for our welfare should come to us from invisible sources, and be conveyed to us from God by unseen hands."[14]

Angels As God's Heavenly Host

In Scripture, angels are often called God's heavenly host. Micaiah the prophet, for example, said, "I saw the LORD sitting on his throne with all the host of heaven standing on his right and on his left" (2 Chronicles 18:18).

The term *host* has a distinctive military ring to it. And indeed, the Bible often portrays the angels as God's host in military fashion. The word "encompasses the whole array of God's heavenly army and sees them employed as a military force to accomplish His will and do His battles. As such, they are an extension of His power and providence."[15]

The great Reformer John Calvin said that angels are called God's host "because, as bodyguards surround their prince, they adorn his majesty and render it conspicuous; like soldiers they are ever intent upon their leader's standard, and thus are ready and able to carry out his commands. As soon as he beckons, they gird themselves for the work, or rather are already at work."[16]

In addition, it is interesting to observe that God is often called the "Lord of hosts" in the Bible. This title "pictures God as the sovereign commander of a great heavenly army, who works all His pleasure in heaven and earth (cf. 1 Samuel 17:45; Psalm 89:6,8 [KJV])."[17] It should give every Christian a supreme sense of security to know that this heavenly army, headed by God Himself, is committed to rendering service to them.

Angels As God's Holy Ones

We noted in an earlier chapter that angels are sometimes called "holy ones" (Job 5:1; 15:15; Psalm 89:7; Daniel 4:13,17,23; 8:13; Jude 14). The word *holy* literally means "set apart." The title "holy ones" is appropriate because God's angels are set apart from sin and set apart unto God's service.

This is in obvious contrast to the fallen angels— demons—who are *un*holy in every way. *They* are set apart from righteousness and set apart unto the Devil to do his unholy bidding. They are against everything related to God.

It is highly significant that the angels, as God's "holy ones," brought the Law to God's chosen people (Acts 7:53; Galatians 3:19; Hebrews 2:2). The Law was given to God's people so that *they themselves* would pursue holiness—that is, so they would be set apart from the pagan nations around them and be set apart unto God. Thus, God used His "holy ones" (angels) as a means of helping His people become holy, too.[18]

Angels As Watchers

In Daniel 4:13 we find reference to angels who are called "watchers." Apparently these are angels who have been sent by God specifically to observe what is transpiring on planet earth. The term suggests that these angels are especially vigilant in their activity of watching the affairs of earth.[19] (The word *watcher*, in biblical Hebrew, communicates the idea of being "vigilant, making sleepless watch."[20]) We might consider the watchers to be God's *reconnaissance agents*.

Some Bible expositors have related the watchers of Daniel 4:13 to other Scripture references that mention the many eyes of certain angels.[21] The cherubim, for example, are described as being "full of eyes" (Ezekiel 1:18). The angels in Revelation 4:6 are likewise described as being "covered with eyes, in front and in back." Verse 8 tells us these angels were "covered with eyes all around, even under [their] wings."

What's in a Title?

We noted at the beginning of this chapter that in ancient times, a name or title was considered to be a statement that revealed something about the person bearing it. We have seen that titles tell us a great deal about the nature and function of angels in God's universe.

To sum up:

• Angels are called *sons of God* because they were directly created by God.

• Angels are called *ministering spirits* because they serve human beings in various ways. They help provide protection, guidance, encouragement, and deliverance.

• Angels are called God's *heavenly host* because they function as God's heavenly army employed as a military force to accomplish His will and engage in His battles.

• Angels are called *holy ones* because they are set apart from sin and set apart unto service to God.

• Some angels are called *watchers* because of their unique role in observing what is transpiring on planet earth.

We learn a lot about angels by the titles used of them in Scripture. But we have yet to look at one extremely important title that comes up quite often in the Old Testament—the Angel of the Lord. In the next chapter, our goal will be to identify this "Angel." I think you'll come to agree with me that the Angel of the Lord is one of the most fascinating topics in the entire Bible.

. . . . .

For even though he [Christ] was not yet clothed with flesh [in Old Testament times], he came down, so to speak, as an intermediary, in order to approach believers more intimately. Therefore this closer intercourse gave him the name of angel.

—John Calvin[1]

·8·

The Angel
of the Lord

One of the most fascinating doctrines in the Old Testament has to do with the identity of the Angel of the Lord. This Angel interacts with such Old Testament luminaries as Abraham, Moses, and David. He plays a very significant role in Old Testament history. But who was he?

Having examined all the verses in the Bible that speak about the Angel of the Lord, I am thoroughly convinced that appearances of this Angel in Old Testament times were actually preincarnate appearances of Jesus Christ, the second person of the Godhead. (*Preincarnate* means "before becoming a human being.") As we examine Scripture together, I think you, too, will come to see that this was no ordinary angel but was in fact the preincarnate Christ.

Theologians call the appearances of Christ in the Old Testament "theophanies." This word comes from two Greek words: *theos* ("God") and *phaino* ("to appear"). We might define a theophany as an appearance or manifestation of God, usually in visible, bodily form. The principal theophany of the Old Testament is the Angel of the Lord (or, more literally, Angel of Yahweh). I believe the Angel of the Lord was the primary manifestation of Christ among people who lived prior to His incarnation.

Now, I need to emphasize that when the word *angel* is used in reference to Christ in the Old Testament, the word indicates not a created being (like other angels) but—true to its Hebrew root—a "messenger," "one who is sent," or "envoy." We will see that Christ, as the Angel of the Lord, was sent by the Father as a messenger or envoy to accomplish specific tasks in Old Testament times. (I'll talk more about the meaning of *angel* later in the chapter.)

How do we know that the Angel of the Lord (or Angel of Yahweh) was actually the preincarnate Christ? We will focus on three lines of evidence in answering this question: 1) this Angel is identified as being Yahweh (or God); 2) though the Angel is identified as being Yahweh, he is also seen to be distinct from another person called Yahweh—thus implying plurality within the Godhead; and 3) the Angel of Yahweh must be Jesus Christ by virtue of what we learn from both the Old and New Testaments about the nature and function of each person in the Trinity.

The Angel of Yahweh Is God

In the Old Testament, the Angel of the Lord makes very definite claims to deity. A well-known example of this is found in the account of Moses and the burning bush: "Moses was tending the flock of Jethro his father-in-law, the priest of Midian, and he led the flock to the far side of the desert and came to Horeb, the mountain of God. There the angel of the LORD appeared to him in flames of fire from within a bush" (Exodus 3:1-2).

Now, notice how the "angel" identified himself to
Moses: "I am the God of your father, the God of Abraham, the God of Isaac and the God of Jacob" (Exodus
3:6a). Upon hearing the Angel's identity, "Moses hid his
face, because he was afraid to look at God" (verse 6b).
Moses no doubt had in mind the Old Testament teaching
that no man can see God and live (Genesis 32:30; Exodus
33:20).

The divine Angel then commissioned Moses to lead
the enslaved Israelites out of Egypt. Moses, in the course
of his conversation with the Angel, clearly expressed a
recognition of divinity: "Moses said *to God* [the Angel of
the Lord], 'Suppose I go to the Israelites and say to them,
"The God of your fathers has sent me to you," and they
ask me, "What is his name?" Then what shall I tell
them?'" (Exodus 3:13, emphasis added).

The Angel then answered with a name that can be
used only of God: "*God* [the Angel of the Lord] said to
Moses, 'I AM WHO I AM. This is what you are to say to the
Israelites: "I AM has sent me to you"'" (Exodus 3:14). It is
hard to conceive of how the Angel could have asserted
His deity in any stronger way!

The Angel's deity is also confirmed in Genesis 22. In
this chapter we find God instructing Abraham, "Take
your son, your only son, Isaac, whom you love, and go to
the region of Moriah. Sacrifice him there as a burnt
offering on one of the mountains I will tell you about"
(verse 2). Just as Abraham was about to slay Isaac, the
divine Angel appeared to him and said, "Do not lay a
hand on the boy . . . . Do not do anything to him. Now I
know that you fear God, because you have not withheld
from me your son, your only son" (verse 12, emphasis
added). Notice that withholding Isaac *from the Angel of the
Lord* is identical to withholding him *from God.*

Beyond actual *claims* to deity, we also find evidences
in the Old Testament that the Angel had the *attributes* of

. . . . .

deity. For example, recall what the Angel said to Moses from the burning bush: "Take off your sandals, for the place where you are standing *is holy ground*" (Exodus 3:5, emphasis added). Of course, the ground was not holy in and of itself. Rather, the holiness was radiating from the divine Angel. His intrinsic holiness required that Moses not defile the surrounding area with his shoes.[2]

The Angel of the Lord also displayed the attributes of *omniscience* (he was all-knowing) and *omnipotence* (he was all-powerful). These attributes are more than evident in the circumstances where the Angel made promises by His own authority that only God could make.[3] For example, after Hagar fled into the desert to escape from Sarah (Abraham's wife), the divine Angel appeared and promised her, "I will so increase your descendants that they will be too numerous to count" (Genesis 16:10).

No ordinary angel could ever make such a promise. After all, the promise itself required the exercise of *omniscience* and fulfilling the promise would require *omnipotence*.[4] Hagar sensed she was in the presence of God, for she was surprised that she was permitted to live after seeing God (Genesis 16:13).

The Angel of the Lord gave other clear evidences of His divine nature. For example, He had the authority to forgive sins (Exodus 23:21), something only God can do. The Angel also received worship (Joshua 5:14; cf. Exodus 3:5) and accepted sacrifices from people (Judges 13:19-23). Moreover, He always spoke and acted in His own intrinsic authority (Genesis 16:10). This is in contrast to created angels, who exist to do the bidding of Christ (Colossians 1:16-17).

There are many other evidences we could look at that prove beyond any doubt the Angel's identity as God. However, the above are sufficient to demonstrate that appearances of the Angel of the Lord (Angel of Yahweh)

. . . . .

in the Old Testament were, in fact, appearances of God. (My book *Christ Before the Manger: The Life and Times of the Preincarnate Christ* goes into great detail on this exciting doctrine.[5])

Despite our certainty on this, however, we have yet to see any indication about whether the Angel was an appearance of the triune God, or, perhaps, one person of the Godhead—the Father, the Son, or the Holy Spirit. We will now begin to narrow the field.

The Angel of Yahweh
Is Distinct from Yahweh

We saw earlier that the Angel of the Lord was recognized as being Yahweh (God). However, the divine Angel is also recognized in Scripture as being *distinct* from another person called Yahweh.

How do we resolve this apparent contradiction? By recognizing Trinitarian distinctions in the Godhead! Though the doctrine of the Trinity is not fully revealed until the New Testament, we nevertheless see preliminary glimpses of this important doctrine in the pages of the Old Testament.

For example, in Zechariah 1:12 we find the Angel of Yahweh interceding to another person called Yahweh on behalf of the people of Jerusalem and Judah: "The angel of the LORD [Yahweh] said, 'LORD [Yahweh] Almighty, how long will you withhold mercy from Jerusalem and from the towns of Judah, which you have been angry with these seventy years?'"

What we have here is *one* person of the Trinity (the second person—the preincarnate Christ as the Angel of the Lord) interceding before *another* person of the Trinity (the first person—God the Father). As a result of this

. . . . .

intercession, the Father reaffirmed His intentions to bless and prosper the chosen people.

We again see Trinitarian distinctions in Zechariah 3:1-2. This passage portrays the Angel of Yahweh calling upon Yahweh. Zechariah witnesses the Angel of Yahweh defending Joshua (the high priest) against the accusations of Satan in the presence of Yahweh. In other words, Zechariah sees an Angel called Yahweh speaking to a separate person also called Yahweh! How can there be two different persons with the name Yahweh? The answer is found in the Trinitarian God. One person in the Trinity (the divine Angel, Jesus Christ) was addressing another person in the Trinity (the Father).[6]

Some people might be tempted to argue that since the Angel of Yahweh is portrayed as interceding to or calling upon Yahweh, He must be less than deity. However, as I point out in *Christ Before the Manger*, the Angel's intercessory prayer to Yahweh and His calling upon Yahweh is no more a disproof of His essential unity with Yahweh than the intercessory prayer of Christ to the Father in John 17 is a disproof of His divinity.[7]

It must be recognized that Christ is often portrayed as interceding to the Father in the New Testament: "He [Jesus] is able to save completely those who come to God [the Father] through him, because he always lives to intercede for them" (Hebrews 7:25, inserts added). In Jesus, "we have one who speaks to the Father in our defense—Jesus Christ, the Righteous One" (1 John 2:1).

So far, then, we have seen that the Angel of Yahweh *is* Yahweh. We have also seen that the Angel of Yahweh is *distinct* from another person called Yahweh. These are important foundational truths (Trinitarian distinctions) to keep in mind as we continue to narrow our focus regarding the precise identity of the divine Angel.

. . . . .

The Angel of the Lord
Is the Preincarnate Christ

How can one person who is clearly identified as God (the Angel of Yahweh) address *another* person who is just as clearly God (Yahweh)? Since there is *only one God,* the answer must lie in the personal distinctions of the Trinity. More specifically, the answer lies in recognizing the Angel of the Lord as the second person of the Trinity, Jesus Christ.

I believe there are a number of fundamental considerations which, when combined, present a strong case for the idea that the Angel of the Lord was actually the preincarnate Christ. Let's take a brief look at five of these considerations.

1. *While Christ is the visible God of the New Testament, neither the Father nor the Holy Spirit characteristically manifest themselves visibly.* It is true that the Father's voice is heard from heaven and the Holy Spirit is seen descending as a dove at Jesus' baptism (Matthew 3:16-17). But only Jesus took on visible, bodily form: "The Word *became flesh* and made his dwelling among us" (John 1:14; cf. Colossians 2:9). It seems reasonable to assume a consistency between the Old and New Testaments, with Christ being the visible manifestation of God in both Testaments.

There are specific statements in the New Testament that would seem to support this view. For one thing, Paul tells us that God the Father is invisible (Colossians 1:15; 1 Timothy 1:17) and "lives in unapproachable light, whom *no one has seen* or can see" (1 Timothy 6:16, emphasis added). John's Gospel likewise tells us that "no one has ever seen God [the Father], but God the One and Only [Jesus Christ], who is at the Father's side, has made him known" (John 1:18, inserts added). John 5:37 similarly tells us that no one has ever seen God the Father's form. These passages indicate that it was the Son's unique function to make the Father, *who has never been seen*, known to man.

Scripture also portrays the Holy Spirit as being invisible to the human eye. In the Upper Room Discourse, for example, Jesus said of the Holy Spirit: "The world cannot accept him, because it neither sees him nor knows him. But you know him, for he lives with you and will be in you" (John 14:17). The invisible Holy Spirit is known by believers because *He indwells them*.

Jesus also said: "The wind blows wherever it pleases. You hear its sound, but you cannot tell where it comes from or where it is going. So it is with everyone born of the Spirit" (John 3:8). The presence of the Holy Spirit is known not by a visible manifestation but by His *effect* on people.[8]

The above facts about the Father and the Holy Spirit point to Christ as being the One who visibly appeared in Old Testament times as the Angel of the Lord.[9] This would seem to be the only interpretation that does full justice to the above Scripture passages.

2. *Just as Christ was sent by the Father in the New Testament, so also was the Angel of Yahweh sent by Yahweh in the Old Testament*. The divine pattern in Scripture is that the Father is the *Sender* and the Son is the *Sent One*.

Of course, this implies no superiority of the Father or inferiority of the Son. This is simply the eternal relationship of the first and second persons of the Trinity. That the Angel and Jesus were both sent by the Father—one in the Old Testament (Judges 13:8-9), the other in the New (John 3:17)—lends support to the idea that they are one and the same person.[10]

3. *Both the Angel of Yahweh in the Old Testament and Christ in the New Testament* interceded to *and* called upon *God the Father*. The New Testament pattern is that the second person of the Trinity, Jesus, consistently

intercedes to the first person, the Father (*see* John 17; Hebrews 7:25; 1 John 2:1). This pattern is never reversed in Scripture (that is, we never see the Father interceding to Jesus). The intercessory ministry of the Angel, then, points us to His identity as the preincarnate Christ.[11]

4. *The divine Angel and Christ engaged in amazingly similar ministries.* Besides interceding for the people of God (Zechariah 1:12-13; 3:1-2; John 17; Romans 8:34; Hebrews 7:25), both the Angel and Christ were involved in *revealing truth* (Daniel 4:13,17,23; 8:16; 9:21; John 1:1,14,18), *commissioning individuals for service* (Exodus 3:7-8; Judges 6:11-23; 13:1-21; Matthew 4:18-20; 28:19-20; Acts 26:14-18), *delivering those enslaved* (Exodus 3; Galatians 1:4; 1 Thessalonians 1:10; 2 Timothy 4:18; Hebrews 2:14-15), *comforting the downcast* (Genesis 16:7-13; 1 Kings 19:4-8; Matthew 14:14; 15:32-39), *protecting God's servants* (Psalm 34:7; Daniel 3:15-25; 6:16-22; Matthew 8:24-26), and *acting as Judge* (1 Chronicles 21:1,14-15; John 5:22; Acts 10:42), among many other things. I believe that these parallel ministries point to the common identity of the Angel and Jesus Christ.

5. *The Angel of the Lord no longer appears after the incarnation.* This is *highly* significant. After reading about the active role played by the Angel throughout Old Testament history, His sudden disappearance after the incarnation would be strange indeed unless He was a preincarnate manifestation of Jesus Christ. There is no other way to explain the Angel's complete inactivity among humans in New Testament times unless He is recognized as *continuing* His activity as *God incarnate*— that is, as Jesus Christ.[12]

Some sharp readers may be thinking, *What about the references (albeit few) in the New Testament to "an angel of the Lord"?* Theologian Norman Geisler explains it this way:

An angel of the Lord (Gabriel) appeared to
Joseph (Matthew 1:20); *an* angel of the Lord
spoke to Philip (Acts 8:26); and *an* angel of
the Lord released Peter (Acts 12:7), but not
the Angel of the Lord. Furthermore, the New
Testament "angel of the Lord," unlike "*the*
Angel of the Lord" in the Old Testament,
did not permit worship of himself (cf. Revelation 22:8-9), but "*the* Angel of the Lord'" in
the Old Testament demanded worship (cf.
Exodus 3:5; Joshua 5:15).[13]

It is exceedingly important to distinguish between
an angel of the Lord in the New Testament (a created
angel) and *the* Angel of the Lord in the Old Testament
(the preincarnate Christ). We must be cautious not to get
confused between the two.

The View of the Early Church

A look at the beliefs of the early church fathers
supports the idea that appearances of the Angel of the
Lord in the Old Testament were actually appearances of
the preincarnate Christ. Irenaeus (A.D. 125-200), a dis-
ciple of Polycarp, said in his *Against Heresies* that Christ
was often seen by Moses and that it was Christ who
spoke to Moses from the burning bush.[14] Irenaeus also
said Christ was "implanted everywhere" throughout
Moses's writings—interacting with such individuals as
Adam, Noah, Abraham, and Jacob.[15]

Church father Justin Martyr (A.D. 110-166) taught
that Christ was extremely active in Old Testament times,
dealing with individuals such as Noah, Abraham, Isaac,
and Jacob. In one of his writings, Martyr said, "Our
Christ conversed with Moses under the appearance of
fire from a bush." It was not God the Father who spoke to

. . . . .

Moses, but "Jesus the Christ," who "is also God," yea, "the God of Abraham, Isaac, and Jacob," and "the I am that I am."[16]

Church father and defender of the faith Tertullian (A.D. 160-220) similarly stated this in *Against Praxeas*:

> It is the Son, therefore, who has been from the beginning administering judgment, throwing down the haughty tower, and dividing the tongues, punishing the whole world by the violence of waters, raining upon Sodom and Gomorrah fire and brimstone, as the LORD from the LORD. For He is who was at all times came down to hold converse with men, from Adam on to the patriarchs and the prophets, in vision, in dream, in mirror, in dark saying.[17]

Other ancient writers who believed that the Angel of the Lord was actually the preincarnate Christ include Clement of Alexandria (A.D. 150-220), Origen (A.D. 185-254), Theophilus of Antioch (died A.D. 181), Cyprian (A.D. 200-258), Hilary (A.D. 315-367), and Saint Basil (A.D. 330-379).[18]

A Clue in the Words of Jesus

Did Jesus speak about His preincarnate appearances to anyone during His ministry on earth? It may very well be that Jesus did just that to the two disciples on the road to Emmaus following His resurrection from the dead: "Beginning with Moses and all the Prophets, he [Christ] explained to them what was said *in all the [Old Testament] Scriptures* concerning Himself" (Luke 24:27, emphasis and inserts added). It seems unlikely that Jesus

. . . . .

spoke to the two disciples *only* about prophecies regarding His coming. We can reasonably assume that He also spoke of His preincarnate appearances.[19]

On another occasion, Jesus told a group of Jews, "If you believed Moses, you would believe me, *for he wrote about me*. But since you do not believe what he wrote, how are you going to believe what I say?" (John 5:46-47, emphasis added). What Moses wrote (Genesis, Exodus, Leviticus, Numbers, and Deuteronomy) includes not only some prophecies about Christ's future incarnation and ministry (for example, Genesis 3:15 and Deuteronomy 18:18), but also some of Christ's preincarnate appearances to humans (for example, Genesis 16:7; 22:11; and Exodus 3).

Thus, some passages in the New Testament point to the real possibility that Jesus indeed spoke about His preincarnate appearances to select individuals.

The Meaning of *Angel*

If it is true that appearances of the Angel of the Lord in Old Testament times were actually preincarnate appearances of Christ, then it is critical that we anchor in our minds the precise sense in which He can properly be called an Angel. I alluded to this earlier, but it bears repeating so that there is no confusion on the matter.

In accordance with its Hebrew root, the word a*ngel* was used of Christ in the sense of "messenger," "one who is sent," or "envoy."[20] This usage indicates that Christ was acting on behalf of the Father. Christ, as the Angel of the Lord, was a divine *intermediary* between God the Father and man.

Famed Reformer John Calvin put it this way: "For even though he [Christ] was not yet clothed with flesh, he came down, so to speak, *as an intermediary*, in order to approach believers more intimately. Therefore this closer

. . . . .

intercourse gave him the name of angel. Meanwhile, what was his he retained, that as God he might be of ineffable glory."[21] Calvin's point is well taken, for even though Christ may have *appeared* in the form of an angel, He would forever retain His intrinsic deity and glory.

ANGELS
A M O N G U S

PART 3

What Angels Do

. . . .

*Even heaven itself has never seen
anything so marvelous as the
incarnation and the suffering and
death of the Creator; nothing so
inconceivable as the complete
redemption of rebels made to become
the church of the Lord.*

—Rene Pache[1]

·9·

Celestial Spectators of Planet Earth

In an earlier chapter we touched on a special class of angels known as *watchers*, whose apparent role it is to observe the affairs of earth (Daniel 4:13). Yet Scripture indicates there is a sense in which *all* angels may be considered celestial spectators of planet earth. Indeed, 1 Peter 1:12 tells us that all the angels "long to look into" things related to God's redemption of humankind. This is a topic of great fascination for the entire angelic realm.[2]

We must remember that angels have been observing earth from the very beginning. They were present when man was first created. They witnessed the temptation and fall of Adam and Eve in the Garden of Eden. Throughout the Old Testament era they witnessed one prophet after another speak forth words regarding the Redeemer who would be born in Bethlehem. They witnessed the incarnation and watched as Christ—the One they had served since their creation—took on human flesh. They also witnessed His cruel execution on the cross of Calvary and His glorious resurrection from the dead. In short, the angels—from the very start—have been celestial spectators of the unfolding drama of human redemption being played out on planet earth. Let's take a closer look at what they saw—and what they will see in the days to come.

Witnessing the Creation and Fall of Man

The angels were present when Adam and Eve were created. They heard their beloved God speak the words, "Let us make man in our image, in our likeness, and let them rule over the fish of the sea and the birds of the air, over the livestock, over all the earth, and over all the creatures that move along the ground" (Genesis 1:26). And they beheld God as He constructed man from the dust of the ground and breathed the breath of life into him (Genesis 2:4-7).[3] How awesome this experience must have been for them!

But their awe soon turned to agony when they witnessed the fall of Adam and Eve in the Garden of Eden. As Arno Gaebelein has so well put it, "With what horror they must have watched when the serpent, Satan, whom they knew so well, sneaked up to the woman and the fatal conversation began. If angels can weep and demons laugh, when sin was born conceived by the liar and murderer from the beginning, angels must have wept in deepest agony, while the demon-world shouted for joy."[4]

Immediately after the Fall, God pronounced judgment against the man, woman, and Satan (the serpent). But as dark and depressing as this situation was, God also introduced a glimmer of hope into the scenario when He spoke to the serpent of the coming Redeemer: "I will put enmity between you and the woman, and between your offspring and hers; he will crush your head, and you will strike his heel" (Genesis 3:15). The "offspring" of the woman, of course, is a reference to Jesus' future birth as a human being, whose work on the

. . . . .

cross would deal a fatal blow to Satan and his dark kingdom.[5]

Ever since that time, the angels have eagerly sought to look into the unfolding drama of human redemption as it is being worked out before their very eyes. From the time they heard the first promise of the Redeemer in Genesis 3:15, they have waited with great anticipation for further words of revelation regarding the promised One. And as God gave revelation, they learned and understood. His unfathomable love towards the lost world of humanity became known to them.

Witnessing the Incarnation

The long-awaited day finally arrived. The anticipated moment had come at last. The angels in heaven surrounded the throne and stood in holy awe as the time came for Jesus—their beloved Creator—to veil His glory and take on the creature's form, to be made a little lower than the angels (Philippians 2:6-11; Hebrews 2:9). They stood in deepest reverence as they beheld Jesus about to leave heaven to come to earth to fulfill all that the prophets of God had spoken.

For the previous 400 years, God had given no new revelation to the chosen people, the Jews. Nor had any angels appeared to humans during this time, so far as we know. But now—with the approaching human birth of the Redeemer—angelic activity would increase dramatically.

We will look at this angelic activity in greater detail in chapter 11, "Ministers to Jesus Christ." For now it is sufficient to note simply that the angel Gabriel informed Zechariah that he and his wife would give birth to John the Baptist, who would prepare the way for the coming Redeemer (Luke 1:13-17). Just a few months later, this same Gabriel was sent from God's throne to announce to

. . . . .

Mary that she would give birth to that promised Redeemer (Luke 1:26-35). No greater news was ever sent from the courts of heaven to the lowly realm of earth. The Redeemer whom the prophets had spoken of for thousands of years was now about to take on human flesh.

Can you imagine the reverential awe among the angels when they finally beheld the Christ-babe born from the womb of Mary? The memorable night had come. The long-expected child was now cradled in a manger in Bethlehem. The seed of the woman had arrived at last. "All heaven was astir that night. The whole universe filled with the angels of God knows what has taken place. The earth alone is in ignorance of the great event."[6]

But this ignorance would not last long. Following the birth of the Redeemer, a glorious angel appeared to some shepherds living out in the fields nearby. He announced to them that the Redeemer had been born (Luke 2:8-11). Not unexpectedly, the news spread like wildfire.

Witnessing Christ's Earthly Ministry

During Christ's earthly ministry there were many people from all different walks of life who believed in Him. What a continual source of joy this was for the angels! Indeed, we are told that the angels in heaven rejoice each time a person places faith in Christ and receives the gift of eternal life (Luke 15:7).

The angels must also have uttered shouts of joy every time Jesus—with His omnipotent power—cast a demon (a fallen angel) out of an enslaved human being. They no doubt smiled every time Jesus brought physical healing to a suffering person. And what holy awe they must have felt when they witnessed Him raising people from the dead!

. . . . .

But there were also other things the angels witnessed that must have been difficult for them to bear. I think of the many people—particularly the religious leaders—who utterly rejected Christ as the Redeemer. I wonder how the angels felt when they saw this. Did they shudder and tremble upon beholding cruel and even hateful denials of the One they loved and served?

Witnessing the Crucifixion

Perhaps most difficult of all, the angels saw Jesus when He was mocked, cruelly scourged, and His face marred and dishonored. Legions of angels likely hovered about Him, wincing in pain as all this occurred. Jesus knew He could have called upon these angels to rescue Him (Matthew 26:53), but the Scriptures had to be fulfilled: *He had to die on the cross.* All heaven must have been affected by what was transpiring on this tiniest of planets in the universe. Creation's Lord was being put to death for the creature's sin!

Finally the work was done. The work of redemption had been completed. And just before His death, Jesus triumphantly cried, "It is finished" (John 19:30). These words must have echoed throughout the entire angelic realm: "It is finished. . . . It is finished. . . . It is finished!" Bible expositor Leon Morris tells us, "This is not the moan of the defeated, nor the sigh of patient resignation. It is the triumphant recognition that He has now fully accomplished the work that He came to do."[7] *It was indeed finished!*

Witnessing the Resurrection and Ascension

Imagine the deafening cheers and applause that must have broken out spontaneously among the angels at the moment of the resurrection. Christ's body had

. . . . .

been dead for three days. Then, at a moment in time, He was alive again—forevermore (Luke 24:1-6).

And as Christ ascended into heaven, it very well may be that thousands of angels accompanied Him en route. Some scholars believe a hint of this may be found in Psalm 68:17-18, which makes reference to the Lord ascending "on high" accompanied by "tens of thousands and thousands of thousands" of angels.

What an awesome moment it must have been when Christ, clothed in a glorified human body, returned to heaven, His natural habitat. What shouts of glory must have then been heard among the cherubim, seraphim, dominions, thrones, powers, and angelic authorities of heaven! A mighty hallelujah chorus no doubt swept through the heavens as He seated Himself "in the heavenly realms, far above all rule and authority, power and dominion, and every title that can be given, not only in the present age but also in the one to come" (Ephesians 1:20,21).[8]

Witnessing the End Times

All the universe is presently in a state of waiting. The spirits of the redeemed in heaven are waiting for that soon-approaching day when they will receive their resurrection bodies—bodies that will be immortal and imperishable (1 Corinthians 15:50-53). On the earth, Christ's church—His Bride—awaits the coming of the divine Groom. Believers on every continent long for His blessed appearing: "Amen. Come Lord Jesus" (Revelation 22:20).

When Christ finally comes again, all heaven will be astir. Imagine the commotion that will take place among the angels in heaven as they gather to return to earth with their beloved Creator. And when Christ and the angels arrive on earth, there will be a splendid display of

. . . . .

glory (Matthew 25:31). "In that day the earth will become the scene of glory as never before in its history. Angels will then be manifested and be seen in their heavenly glory, the invisible things will become visible."[9] What a day that will be!

*God's angels act only to carry out
God's commands. There is no instance
of their acting independently.*

—Millard Erickson[1]

·10·

Servants of the Most High

Time magazine exclaims, "For those who choke too easily on God and his rules...angels are the handy compromise, all fluff and meringue, kind, nonjudgmental. And they are available to everyone, like aspirin."[2] Joan Wester Anderson, author of *Where Angels Walk*, says "angels are a gateway to spirituality for people who find the Judeo-Christian image of God too threatening."[3] Phyllis Tickle, religion editor of *Publishers Weekly*, says that "like ecology, angels allow us a safe place to talk to each other about spiritual things. They provide a socially acceptable way to talk about God without stating a theological commitment."[4]

In today's angel craze, it is the *angels* who are on center stage, not God. God is too threatening, too judgmental, we are told. God demands a commitment. People do not like threats, judgment, and commitment. Angels, it is claimed, do not carry all this baggage—and this explains their popularity, at least in New Age circles.

When we turn to the pages of Scripture, we find that it is always God who is on center stage and that the angels exist *solely* to do His sovereign bidding. In fact, as we will soon discover, they are *never* seen acting independently of God.

It is interesting that in the book of Colossians the apostle Paul gives explicit warnings against angel cults. Apparently, there was a heresy or cult in Colossae that involved the worship of angels. To correct this error, Paul states in Colossians 1:16-17 that Christ is the One who created all things, including all the angels, and hence, He is supreme and is alone worthy to be worshiped.

Later, in Colossians 2:18, Paul sternly warns against the worship of angels.[5] Elsewhere he warned against worshiping the created in place of the Creator (Romans 1:25). Such passages are extremely condemning of today's angel craze, for much of what is going on now certainly constitutes a form of angel worship.

We must keep in mind what the psalmist said: "Who in the skies above can compare with the LORD? Who is like the LORD among the heavenly beings?" (Psalm 89:6). The fact is, there is *no one* like the Lord and *only He* is worthy to be worshiped. There is an infinite distance between God and His angels. To ignore this distance is to fall into great theological folly.

In what follows we will examine some key scriptures regarding angels and their proper relationship to God. In so doing, we will see that much of what is being taught about angels in some of today's bestselling angel books flatly contradicts the Word of God.

Does God *Need* Angels?

God does not *need* angels! In saying this, my intention is not to minimize the importance of what the Bible teaches about angels. I, personally, am very thankful that God created angels. My point is simply that God is

. . . . . .

fully capable of accomplishing His ends without their assistance.

Addressing why God has chosen to use angels to carry out some of His directives in the world, Reformer John Calvin says, "Surely he does not do this out of necessity as if he could not do without them, for as often as he pleases, he disregards them and carries out his work through his will alone."[6] Theologian Charles Ryrie likewise says, "Of course, God is not obliged to use angels; He can do all these things directly. But seemingly He chooses to employ the intermediate ministry of angels on many occasions."[7]

Though God does not need angels, He nevertheless created them—for His own *pleasure* and for His own *glory*—to carry out various functions in *His* universe and before *His* throne. What do these functions involve? Among other things, Scripture indicates that God created angels to minister and evidence God's special concern for us as His children (Hebrews 1:14). Hence, His use of angels does not detract from His personal love and concern for us, but rather is an illustration and expression of it.[8]

Related to the above, Bible scholar Bernard Ramm once made the statement, "We can imagine God as existing without angels, but it is meaningless to imagine a universe with angels but no God."[9] I think Ramm is right (*see* John 1:3; Hebrews 1:2,10).

What is ironic is that in today's angel craze, many people act as if angels exist without there being a personal God. Or, if they acknowledge God's existence, they push Him off of center stage and relegate Him to a place of irrelevance. What these people don't seem to realize is that the holy angels themselves insist on humans recognizing that God alone is to remain on center stage (*see* Revelation 22:8-9).

. . . . . .

Unreserved Service to God

At the start of this chapter I quoted an important statement from theologian Millard Erickson: "God's angels act only to carry out God's commands. There is no instance of their acting independently."[10] Erickson is 100 percent correct. There is not a single Bible verse that portrays an elect, holy angel of God acting independently from God.

Now, in Scripture angels are most often described in relation to God as *His* angels (for example, Psalm 104:4). And it is of great significance that two angelic names mentioned in the Bible—Michael and Gabriel—emphasize this relationship with God with the *el* ending—which, in Hebrew, means "God."[11] (*Michael* means "Who is like God?" and *Gabriel* means "Mighty one of God.") Angels are *God's* angels and they exist to carry out *His* purposes. Psalm 103:20 makes reference to God's angels as those "who do his bidding, who obey his word."

Examples of angels being sent out to accomplish God's will are sprinkled throughout Scripture—from the first book in the Bible to the last. Genesis 19:12-16, for instance, tells us that God sent some angels to destroy the wicked city of Sodom as a judgment. The book of Revelation portrays a number of different angels involved in the outworking of God's sovereign plan in the end times (for example, *see* chapters 8-10).

We must ever keep in mind, then, that angels are always sent to do God's bidding, and there is never any indication that the *sent one* is more significant than the divine *Sender*.[12] God is always the One portrayed as being in total control, not the angels.

Because the angels are always sent by God on our behalf, our gratitude must go to the God who sent them. God's holy angels do not seek praise or worship for the things they do. In fact, they refuse it and point to God as the only one worthy of worship. When the apostle John wrongly bowed down before an angel in an act of worship, the angel said, "Do not do it! I am a fellow servant with you and with your brothers the prophets and of all who keep the words of this book. Worship God!" (Revelation 22:9).

John Calvin said that "as God does not make [the angels] ministers of his power and goodness to share his glory with them, so he does not promise us his help through their ministry in order that we should divide our trust between them and him."[13] Calvin further stated that the angels "do lead us away unless they lead us by the hand straight to him, that we may look upon him, call upon him, and proclaim him as our sole helper; unless we regard them as his hands that are moved to no work without his direction; unless they keep us in the one Mediator, Christ, that we may wholly depend upon him, lean upon him, be brought to him, and rest in him."[14]

How contrary Calvin's sentiments are to some of today's bestselling books about angels. Indeed, the "angels" they speak of *do not* lead us to the God of the Bible.

This brings to mind what the apostle Paul said in 2 Corinthians 11:14: "Satan himself masquerades as an angel of light." The demons who follow him do that as well (verse 15). I am convinced that many of the "angels" who are so popular among New Age angel enthusiasts today are nothing less than demonic spirits who are impersonating angels.

This, of course, is not to downplay or minimize the importance of genuine appearances and activities of the holy angels. I believe such appearances do occur and that angels are very active in our world today. My warning is

. . . . .

simply that when the current angel mania is tested against Scripture (1 Thessalonians 5:21), much of it does not measure up. *Reader beware!*

Glorious Praise and Worship to God

Scripture reveals that a primary function of angels is the worship and praise of Almighty God. In fact, some angels *unceasingly* praise God day and night. Revelation 4:8, for example, tells us, "Each of the four living creatures [angels] had six wings and was covered with eyes all around, even under his wings. Day and night they never stop saying: 'Holy, holy, holy is the Lord God Almighty, who was, and is, and is to come.'"

Scripture gives the distinct impression that the angels give this praise audibly, as they did at the birth of Jesus Christ (Luke 2:13-14).[15] Imagine, then, the glorious sound that greeted the apostle John's ears when he witnessed 100 million angels singing praises in unison to the God they adore:

> I looked and heard the voice of many angels, numbering thousands upon thousands, and ten thousand times ten thousand. They encircled the throne and the living creatures and the elders. In a loud voice they sang: "Worthy is the Lamb, who was slain, to receive power and wealth and wisdom and strength and honor and glory and praise!" (Revelation 5:11-12).

Someday, we who are believers will receive glorified bodies and join in the countless multitude of angels in singing praise to God. That's a day to look forward to!

. . . . .

*If the angels exert such a ministry
in regard to Christ, it is because
they are particularly subordinated to Him.
Like all other creatures, they were
made by Him and for Him.*

—Rene Pache[1]

· 11 ·

Ministers to Jesus Christ

P aul states in Colossians 1:16 that everything in the universe—including the angels—was created *by* Christ and *for* Christ. All things were created for Christ's glory, for such purposes as He sovereignly designed. The universe was built by Him to be His own property, to be the theater in which He could accomplish His purposes and display His infinite perfections.[2]

As we examine what Scripture says about angels, it becomes increasingly clear just what Colossians 1:16 means when it says the angels were created *for* Christ. Indeed, we find numerous occasions in the Bible where the angels are heartily engaged in various duties for Christ or on His behalf.

In this chapter we will take a close look at these duties, which include the worship and praise of Christ, the announcements to both Mary and Joseph regarding Christ's birth, the proclamation of Christ's birth to the shepherds, angelic intervention during the earthly life of Jesus, and angelic involvement at the crucifixion, resurrection, ascension, and second coming of Christ.

Worshiping the Preincarnate Christ

Some 700 years before Christ was born in Bethleham, we find a fascinating account of the angels worshiping Him in His preincarnate state. We read about this glorious event in chapter 6 of the book of Isaiah. There, we are told that while Isaiah was in the Temple, he had a vision in which he found himself in the presence of God's glory:

> In the year that King Uzziah died, I saw the Lord seated on a throne, high and exalted, and the train of his robe filled the temple. Above him were seraphs [angels], each with six wings: With two wings they covered their faces, with two they covered their feet, and with two they were flying. And they were calling to one another: "Holy, holy, holy is the LORD Almighty; the whole earth is full of his glory."
>
> At the sound of their voices the doorposts and thresholds shook and the temple was filled with smoke. "Woe to me!" I cried. "I am ruined! For I am a man of unclean lips, and I live among a people of unclean lips, and my eyes have seen the King, the LORD Almighty" (Isaiah 6:1-5).

This passage is rich in meaning. We find the prophet Isaiah in the Temple in 740 B.C., perhaps mourning the death of godly King Uzziah. Isaiah may have gone there to pray in his grief.

While in the Temple, God granted Isaiah a glorious vision that would give him strength for the duration of his ministry. The prophet saw the Lord seated on a throne, "high and exalted" (Isaiah 6:1) and adorned in a long and flowing robe that pointed to His kingly majesty. Though an earthly king had died, the true King of the universe still reigned supreme from on high.

Isaiah saw "seraphs" above God's throne (Isaiah 6:2-3). These were magnificent angels who proclaimed God's holiness and glory. As we noted earlier, the term *seraph* comes from a root word meaning "to burn," emphasizing the burning passion of these angelic beings to serve their King.

These angels covered their faces with their wings in God's presence. Despite their own brightness and purity, they apparently could not look at the greater brightness and purity of God, who—as the New Testament tells us—dwells in "unapproachable light" (1 Timothy 6:16).

The seraphs proclaimed, "Holy, holy, holy is the LORD Almighty" (Isaiah 6:3). Triple repetition is often used in Scripture to emphasize a truth, and in this case, it points to the fullness or completeness of God's holiness.

At the sound of the angels' voices, the doorposts and the thresholds shook and the Temple was filled with smoke (Isaiah 6:4). Human encounters with God often involved the presence of smoke (*see* Exodus 20:18-19). This smoke was no doubt the cloud of glory that Isaiah's ancestors had seen in the wilderness (Exodus 13:21; 16:10) and which the priests in Solomon's day had viewed in the Temple upon its dedication (1 Kings 8:10-13).

All this becomes extremely significant when we go to John's Gospel and read that what Isaiah actually saw was Jesus' glory (John 12:41). The words of Isaiah 6:3 refer to the glory of "the LORD Almighty" (or, more literally, the *Yahweh of hosts*), but John says these words were actually in reference to Jesus Christ. Jesus and Yahweh are here equated.

. . . . .

How awesome this must have been for Isaiah! About 700 years before the Messiah was born in Bethlehem, Isaiah saw the glory of the preincarnate Christ in a vision. And the One whom Isaiah had personally encountered in this vision is the same One whose birth he prophesied (Isaiah 4:2; 7:14; 9:6-7; 11:1-5,10; 32:1; 42:1-4; 49:1-7; 52:13-53:12; 61:1-3). The One Isaiah beheld in this vision—worshiped by the holy angels—is the same One who would be served by those same angels when He became a human being in Bethlehem.

Announcing the Birth to Mary

For several hundred years, God's voice through the prophets had been silent in Palestine. The Roman army had nearly crushed the Jews' hopes that the promised Messiah would come to deliver them. Had God forgotten His people? Many people might have thought so. But when the proper time came, something glorious happened. An angel from heaven appeared to Mary with some incredible news.

The first chapter of Luke's Gospel tells us about this annunciation (announcement):

> In the sixth month, God sent the angel Gabriel to Nazareth, a town in Galilee, to a virgin pledged to be married to a man named Joseph, a descendant of David. The virgin's name was Mary. The angel went to her and said, "Greetings, you who are highly favored! The Lord is with you" (verses 26-28).

Earlier in man's history, the angel Gabriel had given Daniel special revelations from God regarding the coming Messiah (Daniel 8:16; 9:21). Now, over 500 years

. . . . .

later, this same angel appeared to Mary with the news that the promised Messiah would be born by her, a virgin. This was in fulfillment of Isaiah 7:14, which prophesied that the Messiah would be born of a virgin.

Following Gabriel's announcement, Mary was "greatly troubled at his words and wondered what kind of greeting this might be" (Luke 1:29). Apparently, in her modesty and humility, Mary did not understand why a glorious heavenly angel would come to greet her in such exalted terms and tell her that the Lord was with her.

Gabriel then said, "Do not be afraid, Mary, you have found favor with God. You will be with child and give birth to a son, and you are to give him the name Jesus. He will be great and will be called the Son of the Most High. The Lord God will give him the throne of his father David, and he will reign over the house of Jacob forever; his kingdom will never end" (Luke 1:30-33).

Although Gabriel calmed Mary's initial fears, his message probably created additional concerns for her. Would Joseph believe the impossible? What would their friends and neighbors think when they learned that Mary was pregnant? Would she be branded as the worst of sinners rather than God's chosen instrument? Perhaps those questions went through her mind as the heavenly angel spoke to her. Through it all, however, Mary's attitude was one of faith and obedience.

Gabriel's pronouncement that the child would be called *Jesus* is full of meaning. The name *Jesus* means "the Lord saves" or "the Lord is salvation." The name points to the very reason that Christ became a human being—*to save His people.*

Besides informing Mary of the Savior's name, Gabriel also told her that Jesus would be great; He would be called the Son of the Most High; and He would reign on the throne of His father David. Each of these three descriptions are highly revealing of Jesus' true identity. For example, the term "great" is a title which, when unqualified, is usually reserved for God alone.[3]

Being called "the Son of the Most High" is significant, for "Most High" is a title often used of God in both the Old and New Testaments (for example, Genesis 14:19; 2 Samuel 22:14; Psalm 7:10; Acts 7:48). Bible expositor John A. Martin suggests:

> Mary could not have missed the significance of that terminology. The fact that her Baby was to be called the "Son of the Most High" pointed to His equality with God. In Semitic thought a son was a 'carbon copy' of his father, and the phrase "son of" was often used to refer to one who possessed his "father's" qualities.[4]

This "great" one—eternal God in human flesh—would rule, according to Gabriel, on the throne of David. Jesus, who in His humanity was a direct descendant of David (Matthew 1:1), will rule from David's throne during the future 1,000-year millennial kingdom in which there will be perfect righteousness and peace (2 Samuel 7:16; Psalm 89:3-4,28-37). This kingdom will be inaugurated immediately following the second coming of Christ (Revelation 19).

Three words were used by Gabriel in Luke 1:32-33 to describe this future rule of Christ: "throne," "house," and "kingdom" ("The Lord God will give him the *throne* of his father David, and he will reign over the *house* of Jacob forever; his *kingdom* will never end" [emphasis added]). It is significant that each of these words is found in the covenant that God made with David—a covenant in which God promised that someone from David's line would rule forever (2 Samuel 7:16).

. . . . .

Gabriel's words must have brought these Old Testament promises to mind for Mary, who was a devout young Jew. Indeed, Gabriel's message constituted "an announcement as clear as it was possible to make it that Mary's son would come into this world to fulfill the promise given to David that one of David's sons would sit on David's throne and rule over David's kingdom."[5] Jesus would come not only to be the Savior but also to be the Sovereign.

Mary then responded to Gabriel by inquiring, "How will this be . . . since I am a virgin?" (Luke 1:34). The angel answered, "The Holy Spirit will come upon you, and the power of the Most High will overshadow you. So the holy one to be born will be called the Son of God. Even Elizabeth your relative is going to have a child in her old age, and she who was said to be barren is in her sixth month. For nothing is impossible with God" (verses 35-37). Though Mary had not asked Gabriel for a sign, he pointed toward evidence that God's power was already at work by mentioning Mary's relative Elizabeth, who had long been barren but was now pregnant with John the Baptist in her womb.

How overwhelming the announcement of the incarnation must have been for young Mary! It is impossible to know the kinds of emotions she must have felt at the moment of Gabriel's revelation that eternal God would be in her womb. But Mary responded in a humble manner: "I am the Lord's servant," she said. "May it be to me as you have said" (Luke 1:38).

In her heart, Mary may have quietly prayed, "My life's priorities have suddenly been changed. My wedding plans must be laid aside. I am willing to face shame and ridicule. Whatever You say, Lord, I accept."

. . . . .

Announcing the Birth to Joseph

When Joseph discovered that Mary was pregnant, he had two options available to him, neither of which was marriage. (As a righteous man, it was inconceivable to him that he would marry a woman who was carrying what he then presumed to be another man's child.) One option was to publicly accuse Mary of immorality and have her stoned to death (Deuteronomy 22:13-21). Her death would then have served to break the betrothal contract. A second alternative open to Joseph was to divorce Mary (breaking a betrothal required a divorce). Because Joseph was a righteous man and did not want to expose Mary to public disgrace, he decided to divorce her quietly (Matthew 1:19).

But then an angel appeared to Joseph in a dream and informed him that the baby in Mary's womb was of the Holy Spirit (Matthew 1:20).[6] This was no earthly conception or pregnancy, he was told. What had been planned in eternity past was now being fulfilled in his wife-to-be. The angel said, "She will give birth to a son, and you are to give him the name Jesus, because he will save his people from their sins" (Matthew 1:21). In the original Greek text, the last part of this verse is especially emphatic: "It is He and no other who will save His people from their sins."

The angel's revelation to Joseph was necessary because Mary was in a humanly impossible situation. She knew she had been faithful to Joseph, yet she had also submitted to God's will to make her the human mother of the divine-human Messiah. There was no way she could have adequately explained to Joseph what had happened. Thus God sent an angel to Joseph to explain what was going on. The angel's announcement served to defend Mary's moral integrity so that Joseph could marry her in good conscience.

. . . . .

When Joseph awoke from the dream, he did as the angel had commanded him and took Mary home as his wife. Joseph willingly violated Jewish custom by immediately taking her into his home rather than waiting until the one-year betrothal period had passed. However, as the Bible tells us, "he had no union with her until she gave birth to a son. And he gave him the name Jesus" (Matthew 1:25). That Joseph "had no union" with Mary until Jesus was born emphasizes that there was no human causation involved in the fathering of Jesus.[7]

Like Mary, Joseph must have been overwhelmed by the revelation he had received from the angel. The Messiah would be born from his wife's womb! "The eternal Son of the eternal God had existed as One with the Father from all eternity. The One who by his power had created the universe would come in human flesh through Mary's womb. Jesus Christ, the eternal One, reached out through his birth and took to himself a true and complete humanity. He united true humanity and true deity in one person forever. Such was the revelation given to Joseph."[8]

Proclaiming the Arrival to the Shepherds

In dire contrast to Jesus' intrinsic glory and majesty, He was born in lowly conditions and placed in a manger. But His majesty was acknowledged in other ways. Following His birth, a glorious angel appeared to some shepherds living out in the fields nearby to make an announcement of monumental importance—*the Messiah had been born.*

It is hard to imagine what it must have been like as the darkness of the night was suddenly dissipated by the glorious appearance of this angel. Understandably, the shepherds were "terrified" at what they beheld (Luke 2:9).

The angel immediately comforted them and told them not to be afraid. After all, he had come not as a minister of death but as a proclaimer of life to "all the people" (Luke 2:10). This recalls Genesis 12:3, which declares the prophetic announcement that "all peoples on earth" would be blessed through the coming of the Messiah.

The angel then made an astonishing statement: "Today in the town of David [Bethlehem] a Savior has been born to you; he is Christ the Lord" (Luke 2:11). Now, keep in mind that according to the Old Testament, God and *only God* is the Savior of His people. God said, "I, even I, am the LORD, and apart from me there is no Savior" (Isaiah 43:11). And in Luke 2:11, Christ the babe is called "Savior." This is a powerful testimony to Christ's identity as God.

Note that the angel told the shepherds that "Christ *the* Lord" had been born, not "Christ *your* Lord." Christ is the Sovereign not just of men *but of angels as well*.[9] Christ is the Lord, in an unqualified sense, over *all* creation (Colossians 1:16).

As the angel continued speaking to the shepherds, suddenly and without warning "a great company of the heavenly host appeared with the angel, praising God and saying, 'Glory to God in the highest, and on earth peace to men on whom his favor rests'" (Luke 2:13-14). These angels had known and served Christ in His preincarnate state. And now, following the virgin birth, they praised God because the One they had known and served for so long had just been born as a human being—a tiny babe in Bethlehem.

After the angels departed into heaven, the shepherds said to one another, "Let's go to Bethlehem and see this thing that has happened" (Luke 2:15). It is not easy to convey in English the sense of urgency that is present

in the original Greek text of this verse. We might para-
phrase it, "Come on, let us make haste and quickly go
and see."[10] The shepherds were excited about the angel's
message, no doubt partly because of the widespread
messianic expectations in first-century Judaism. They
knew a Messiah was coming, but now they had received
word that He was here!

After the shepherds saw the divine babe, "they
spread the word concerning what had been told them
about this child, and all who heard it were amazed at
what the shepherds said to them" (Luke 2:17-18). The
Greek word for *amaze* means "to wonder," "to be aston-
ished." The word conveys the idea that when people
heard the testimony of the shepherds, they got goose
bumps on their skin and tingles down their spines. The
prophesied Messiah had now come—*eternal God in
human flesh!*

Ministering to Christ on Earth

The Gospel accounts indicate that the holy angels
were very active in ministering to Jesus in various ways
throughout His earthly life.

The Early Infancy of Christ. The first instance of
angelic intervention relates to evil King Herod's desire to
put an end to baby Jesus' life. Herod did not want any
competitors to his throne. His goal, therefore, was to
remove any possibility of a future "King of the Jews." He
wanted to put Jesus to death.

To foil Herod's attempt at killing Jesus, an angel
appeared to Joseph and instructed the family to flee to
Egypt. Joseph at once obeyed the command and went to
Egypt, where he and his family remained until the evil
Herod died (Matthew 2:13-18).

Following Herod's death, an angel appeared to
Joseph in a dream and said, "Get up, take the child and

his mother and go to the land of Israel, for those who were trying to take the child's life are dead" (Matthew 2:20). So Joseph took his family back to the land of Israel, where Jesus was raised.

What can we learn from this account? First, God—in His omniscience—knows the hearts, desires, and plans of all men, including evil rulers like Herod. And second, the angels carried out the sovereign bidding of God by communicating messages and warnings to Joseph and his family. God the Father undertook the providential care of His Son during His infancy through the ministry of angels.

The Early Ministry of Christ. Jesus' public ministry was inaugurated at His baptism in the River Jordan (Matthew 3). Following His baptism, He was led into the desert to be tempted by the Devil (Matthew 4:1). Satan's purpose in tempting Jesus was to thwart God's plan of redemption by disqualifying the Savior. But God's purpose was to prove that Jesus was sinless and was thus a worthy Savior.

Scripture tells us that following the temptations, "the devil left him, and angels came and attended him" (Matthew 4:11). The word "attended" comes from a Greek word meaning "to serve," "wait upon," "care for someone's needs."[11] This is what the angels did for Jesus. Following this 40-day period of intense temptations, the angels served Him, waited upon Him, and cared for His needs.

At Gethsemane. Just prior to His arrest the night before His crucifixion, Jesus was in the Garden of Gethsemane feeling the tremendous weight of what was ahead of Him. After He prayed to the Father, an angel appeared from heaven and "strengthened" Him (Luke 22:43). The word "strengthened" in this verse literally means "to invigorate," "cause to be strong," "to make firm."[12] This angel performed a vital ministry for Christ just prior to His going to the cross to die for the sins of humankind.

At the Crucifixion. During the arrest in the garden, one of the disciples drew a sword to defend Jesus. But Jesus responded by saying, "Do you think I cannot call on my Father, and he will at once put at my disposal more than twelve legions of angels?" (Matthew 26:53). A Roman legion had 6,000 soldiers; Twelve legions of angels would thus amount to 72,000 angels.

Jesus' point, of course, was that if He so desired, He could have called upon innumerable angels to deliver Him. But He chose not to do this so He could go to the cross and secure salvation for humankind. Commenting on this, evangelist Billy Graham said,

> The angels would have come to the cross to rescue the King of kings, but because of His love for the human race and because He knew it was only through His death that they could be saved, He refused to call for their help. The angels were under orders not to intervene at this terrible, holy moment. Even the angels could not minister to the Son of God at Calvary. He died alone in order to take the full death penalty you and I deserved.[13]

Serving at the Resurrection

After Jesus had died on the cross, His body was buried in accordance with Jewish burial customs. He was wrapped in a linen cloth, and about 100 pounds of aromatic spices—mixed together to form a gummy substance—were applied to the wrappings of cloth around Him.

After His body was placed in a solid-rock tomb, an extremely large stone was rolled against the entrance with the help of levers. This stone would have weighed up to four tons (8,000 pounds). It is not a stone that would have been easily moved by human beings.

Roman guards were then stationed at the tomb. These strictly disciplined men were highly motivated to succeed in all they were assigned by the Roman government. Fear of cruel punishment produced flawless attention to duty, especially in the night watches. These Roman guards would have affixed the Roman seal on the tomb, a stamp representing Rome's sovereign power and authority.

All this security at the tomb makes the situation following Christ's resurrection highly significant. The Roman seal had been broken, an offense that carried an automatic penalty of crucifixion upside down for the person who did it. Moreover, the large stone was now a substantial distance from the entrance, as if it had been plucked out of the way like a pebble. The Roman guards had also fled. Since the penalty for a Roman guard leaving his position was death, we can assume they must have had a good reason for fleeing!

We learn the details of what happened in Matthew 28:1-6:

> After the Sabbath, at dawn on the first day of the week, Mary Magdalene and the other Mary went to look at the tomb. There was a violent earthquake, for an angel of the Lord came down from heaven and, going to the tomb, rolled back the stone and sat on it. His appearance was like lightning, and his clothes were white as snow. The guards were so afraid of him that they shook and became like dead men.

. . . . .

The angel said to the women, "Do not be afraid, for I know that you are looking for Jesus, who was crucified. He is not here; he has risen, just as he said."

The rest is history. The women, filled with joy, ran to tell the disciples the glorious news: *Christ has risen!*

Appearing at the Ascension

Christ ascended into heaven before the very eyes of some of His disciples (Acts 1:9). Just as He was ascending, two angels appeared to the disciples and said, "Men of Galilee... why do you stand here looking into the sky? This same Jesus, who has been taken from you into heaven, will come back in the same way you have seen him go into heaven" (verse 11). The angels—as messengers of God—indicated to the disciples that just as Jesus had *visibly* and *physically* ascended into heaven, so also would He *visibly* and *physically* come again at the Second Coming.

Descending at the Second Coming

Scripture consistently tells us that when Christ visibly and physically returns to earth, He will be accompanied by a vast host of angels. Matthew 16:27 says that "the Son of Man is going to come in his Father's glory *with his angels.*" Matthew 25:31 tells us, "When the Son of Man comes in his glory, *and all the angels with him,* he will sit on his throne in heavenly glory." Second Thessalonians 1:7 speaks of Christ coming again "in blazing fire *with his powerful angels.*" What a resplendently glorious scene this will be!

. . . . .

Exalting Christ for All Eternity

Earlier we touched on the fact that angels are involved in the worship of Christ. One of the most glorious Scripture passages dealing with this is Revelation 5:11-14. It is appropriate that we close this chapter with these words from the apostle John:

> I looked and heard the voice of many angels, numbering thousands upon thousands, and ten thousand times ten thousand. They encircled the throne and the living creatures and the elders. In a loud voice they sang: "Worthy is the Lamb, who was slain, to receive power and wealth and wisdom and strength and honor and glory and praise!"
> Then I heard every creature in heaven and on earth and under the earth and on the sea, and all that is in them, singing: "To him who sits on the throne and to the Lamb be praise and honor and glory and power, for ever and ever!" The four living creatures said, "Amen," and the elders fell down and worshiped.

Believers, look up—take courage.
The angels are nearer than you think.

—Billy Graham[1]

·12·

Angels Among **Us**

The angels are nearer than you think. They're all around us, taking care of us and ministering to us when we're not even aware of their presence. What comfort we as believers can gain from this inspiring biblical teaching!

There is a vast world of intelligent, powerful, invisible spirit-beings all around us that warrants careful study. By understanding what Scripture says about the doctrine of angels, believers become aware of one of the most exciting ways God takes care of us during our earthly sojourns.

It is absolutely essential, of course, that we base our understanding of this subject on Scripture. The Reformer John Calvin once said that the error in much angelology is that it deals with angels *apart from* the biblical witness.[2] This is precisely what has happened on a popular level today. Many of the bestselling angel books of our day contain legend, lore, and outright occultism in regard to angels, but pay little attention to what God's Word teaches on the subject.

In this chapter our goal will be to seek an understanding of what *Scripture* says about some of the important ways God uses angels to minister to believers. In the process, my hope and prayer is that your faith in God and His mighty provisions for your life may be strengthened.

The Ministry of Angels to Believers

Hebrews 1:14, as we have noted earlier, says that angels are "ministering spirits sent to serve those who will inherit salvation." But in *what ways* do angels minister to the heirs of salvation?

Among many other things, angels may be utilized by God in answering a believer's prayer (Acts 12:7); sometimes they give encouragement in times of danger (Acts 27:23-24); and they take care of believers at the moment of death (Luke 16:22; Jude 9). The ministry of angels to believers is wide and varied.

John Wesley, the eighteenth-century founder of Methodism, wrote that angels serve humankind "in a thousand ways . . . . They may assist us in our searching after truth, remove many doubts and difficulties . . . they may warn us of evil in disguise, and place what is good in a clear strong light."[3]

Because angels are so active in the believer's life, evangelist Billy Graham says "every true believer in Christ should be encouraged and strengthened! Angels are watching; they mark your path. They superintend the events of your life and protect the interest of the Lord God, always working to promote His plans and to bring about His highest will for you."[4] Indeed, Graham says, if we "would only realize how close His ministering angels are, what calm assurance we could have in facing the cataclysms of life. While we do not place our faith directly in angels, we should place it in the God who rules the angels; then we can have peace."⁵

Let us be clear on this: There are many millions of angels who are at God's command to render service to the heirs of salvation. Indeed, "the hosts of heaven stand at attention as we make our way from earth to glory, and Satan's BB guns are no match for God's heavy artillery."⁶

God's Invisible Helpers

Most people generally walk *by sight* and not *by faith*—that is, they live their lives and interpret reality according to what is tangibly real to their physical senses. Of course, if we limit our understanding of reality to the physical world, then we remain in ignorance regarding the vast world of invisible spirit-beings around us.

We see a number of examples in the Bible that illustrate how angels are often not perceived by humans. Recall that when an angel stopped Balaam, it was at first only the donkey that saw him standing with a drawn sword in his hand (Numbers 22:23,31). The Lord had to "open" Balaam's eyes before he could see the angel.

Another example relates to the prophet Elisha and his servant. Second Kings 6:15-17 tells us:

> When the servant of the man of God got up and went out early the next morning, an army with horses and chariots had surrounded the city. "Oh, my lord, what shall we do?" the servant asked. "Don't be afraid," the prophet answered. "Those who are with us are more than those who are with them." And Elisha prayed, "O LORD, open his eyes so he may see." Then the LORD opened the servant's eyes, and he looked and saw the

hills full of horses and chariots of fire all round Elisha.

Elisha alone perceived the presence of the heavenly host that had come to help him. He had to pray and ask God to reveal the angels to his frightened servant. Like the servant, you and I may often be unaware of the presence of angels in our midst. There is no telling just how many times God has kept us safe through the work of angels without us having known anything about it.

As Billy Graham so aptly put it, "Often [angels] may be our companions without our being aware of their presence. We know little of their constant ministry. The Bible assures us, however, that one day our eyes will be unscaled to see and know the full extent of the attention angels have given us (1 Corinthians 13:11,12)."[7]

God's Messengers

We noted earlier in this book that the word *angel* literally carries the meaning, "messenger." This points to a primary role of the angels. They serve as God's messengers—bringing revelation, announcements, warnings, and other information to the people of God.

Angels appeared to Lot to warn him about the impending judgment on Sodom (Genesis 19). An angel appeared to the prophet Daniel to reveal the future (Daniel 9). An angel appeared to Zechariah to announce the coming birth of John the Baptist (Luke 1:13). Angels appeared to Joseph and Mary to announce the birth of the Savior, Jesus Christ (Matthew 1; Luke 1). An angel appeared to Cornelius and instructed him to send for Simon Peter so Peter could tell him all about salvation in Jesus Christ (Acts 10:3-33). All throughout the pages of Scripture, we find angels appearing to human beings as God's messengers.[8]

. . . . .

Sometimes when bringing a message to a person, angels will take on the appearance of a human being. "The angels are spirits; but in order to communicate with men, they clothe themselves with a human aspect. Sometimes when they appear, they are even taken for men at the beginning; then they reveal their identity as they accomplish their mission."[9] Thus it is that in showing hospitality, believers have in some cases "entertained angels unawares" (Hebrews 13:2 KJV).

Guardians of God's People

Without doubt the most popular and controversial aspect of the study of angels has to do with their role as the guardians of God's people. Some Bible scholars say every single believer has a specific assigned guardian angel who stays with him or her throughout life, while others believe that angels in general are assigned to watch over believers in general.

There are two primary passages in the New Testament that relate to the idea of guardian angels. Matthew 18:10 says, "See that you do not look down on one of these little ones. For I tell you that their angels in heaven always see the face of my Father in heaven." Then, in Acts 12:15, we find a servant girl named Rhoda recognizing Peter's voice outside the door of the house, and the people inside—thinking Peter was still in jail—saying, "You're out of your mind. . . . It must be his angel." A number of theologians have concluded from these two verses that every believer must have his or her own guardian angel.

Many of the early church fathers, for example, believed that every individual is under the care of a particular angel who is assigned to him or her as a guardian. Likewise, the great philosopher and theologian Thomas Aquinas said that each person has a guardian angel assigned to him or her at birth. Prior to the birth of the child, Aquinas said, the child in the womb falls under the care of the mother's guardian angel.[10]

The idea of individual guardian angels for each person is particularly popular today among New Age angel enthusiasts. The line of thinking here is that not just Christians have individual guardian angels, but that *all people on earth* have guardian angels—regardless of whether they believe in the Christ of the Bible.

Why have guardian angels become so popular today? Writer David Connolly offers this answer:

> Human life is often mysterious and frightening, and there is sometimes a profound need in us for a belief in attentive caring and protection greater than what can come from ourselves alone—an inner security gently extended from a higher love and wisdom to sustain us through the fears and dangers of human experience.[11]

Perhaps many today want to believe in guardian angels because it gives them a sense of security in an often chaotic and crime-ridden world.

Of course, the Scriptures teach that angels are ministering spirits not to those who reject Christ but to the "heirs of salvation" (Christians) (Hebrews 1:14). This verse alone causes the New Age view of guardian angels to crumble like a house of cards.

Based upon Matthew 18:10 and Acts 12:15, it is certainly *possible* that each believer has a specific guardian angel assigned to him or her. However, many theologians argue that this is flimsy support for such an idea.[12] (For example, they point out that the angels of the little ones in Matthew 18:10 are said to be *in heaven*, not specifically *with* the little ones.[13]) These theologians argue that Scripture seems to indicate that *many multitudes of angels* are always ready and willing to render help and protection to each individual Christian whenever there is a need. Perhaps Reformer John Calvin put it best:

> Whether individual angels have been assigned to individual believers for their protection, I dare not affirm with confidence. . . . Specific angels have been appointed as guardians over kingdoms and provinces. Christ also, when he says that the children's angels always behold the Father's face [Matthew 18:10], hints that there are certain angels to whom their safety has been committed. But from this I do not know whether one ought to infer that each individual has the protection of his own angel. We ought to hold as a fact that the care of each one of us is not the task of one angel only, but all with one consent watch over our salvation.[14]

Calvin believes that we should feel happy and confident knowing that many angels are constantly guarding us, rather than feel discouraged because we don't each have an individual angel:

> If the fact that all the heavenly host are keeping watch for his safety will not satisfy a man, I do not see what benefit he could derive from knowing that *one* angel has been given to him as his special guardian. Indeed, those who confine to one angel the care that God takes of each one of us are doing a great

. . . . .

injustice both to themselves and to all the members of the church.[15]

Calvin says God "not only promises to take care of us, but tells us he has innumerable guardians whom he has bidden to look after our safety; that so long as we are hedged about by their defense and keeping, whatever perils may threaten, we have been placed beyond all chance of evil."[16] Indeed, he says, "Angels are dispensers and administrators of God's beneficence toward us....They keep vigil for our safety, take upon themselves our defense, direct our ways, and take care that some harm may not befall us."[17] The angels "are ever ready to bring help to us with incredible swiftness, should circumstance require it, even as lightning sent forth from heaven flies to us with its usual speed."[18]

The idea that many angels watch after us seems to have some support in Scripture. For example, we read in 2 Kings 6:17 that Elisha and his servant were surrounded by *many* glorious angels. Luke 16:22 indicates that several angels were involved in carrying Lazarus's soul to Abraham's bosom. Jesus could have called on 12 legions of angels to rescue Him if He had wanted (Matthew 26:53). Psalm 91:9-11 tells us, "If you make the Most High your dwelling—even the LORD, who is my refuge—then no harm will befall you, no disaster will come near your tent. For he will command *his angels* concerning you to guard you in all your ways" (emphasis added).

Whether each of us has just one angel watching over us or many, we cannot say for sure. Yet one thing is certain: If we as Christians were more fully aware of God's provision of angelic protection (regardless of how many angels are involved), we would most certainly be less fearful of our circumstances and enemies. Our big problem, of course, is that we tend to walk by sight and not by faith. The walk of faith is a walk that recognizes God's constant provision of angelic protection.[19]

Ministers Who Answer Prayer

Certainly God does not have to depend upon angels in order to answer the prayers of His people. In fact, oftentimes He *does* answer prayers apart from any angelic involvement (for example, 1 Chronicles 5:20; 1 Peter 3:12). Nevertheless, it is sometimes God's sovereign choice to use angels in answering people's prayers.

One example of this is in Acts 12, where we find Peter wrongfully imprisoned. We read that while Peter was in jail, "the church was earnestly praying to God for him" (verse 5). What happened next? All of a sudden, an angel appeared in Peter's prison cell and helped him escape:

> He struck Peter on the side and woke him up. "Quick, get up!" he said, and the chains fell off Peter's wrists. Then the angel said to him, "Put on your clothes and sandals." And Peter did so. "Wrap your cloak around you and follow me," the angel told him. Peter followed him out of the prison, but he had no idea that what the angel was doing was really happening; he thought he was seeing a vision. They passed the first and second guards and came to the iron gate leading to the city. It opened for them by itself, and they went through it. When they had walked the length of one street, suddenly the angel left him (Acts 12:7-10).

Clearly, here is an example of Christians praying to God and God immediately responding by sending an angel to grant the request. We must assume that God sometimes answers *our* prayers in this way as well. When we petition the throne of God with a prayer request, God may sovereignly grant that request, assigning a specific angel to bring it about.

Related to this, it is important that we be aware that demons (fallen angels) sometimes seek to thwart the angels God uses in the process of answering a particular prayer. We read about one such incident in the book of Daniel.

According to Daniel 10:13, an angel that had been sent by God to answer Daniel's prayer was detained by a more powerful fallen angel (a demon). It was only when the archangel Michael showed up to render aid that the lesser angel was freed to carry out his task. One lesson we learn from this account is that we must be fervent in our prayers and not think that God is not listening simply because there seems to be a delay in God's answer.

Escorts at the Moment of Death

Death has been called "the great equalizer." Regardless of whether a person is a man or a woman, rich or poor, fat or thin, black or white, *all* humans are equal in that they eventually die.

For the Christian, God has taken the sting out of death (1 Corinthians 15:55). Because of what Christ has accomplished for us, death is simply a transition during which our spirits leave our physical bodies and enter directly into the presence of Christ. In a way, then, death is a glorious event.

Perhaps one of the most meaningful ministries angels have to us as believers is that at the very moment of death, they accompany us into heaven (Luke 16:22). When that glorious separation takes place, the angels are there to personally escort us into our eternal inheritance.[20]

As one writer says, "Death for the Christian cuts the cord that holds us captive in this present evil world so that angels may transport believers to their heavenly inheritance."[21] The angels will give the believer a royal welcome as he or she enters the presence of God.

Evangelist Billy Graham reports that when his maternal grandmother died, the room seemed to fill with a heavenly light:

> She sat up in bed and almost laughingly said, 'I see Jesus. He has His arms outstretched toward me. I see Ben [her husband who had died some years earlier] and I see the angels.' She slumped over, absent from the body but present with the Lord.[22]

Graham goes on to describe the glory of what awaits the believer in the next life:

> The wonders, beauties, splendor, and grandeur of heaven will be yours. You will be surrounded by these heavenly messengers sent by God to bring you home where you may rest from your labors, though the honor of your works will follow you (Revelation 14:13).[23]

That will be a glorious day.

An Awesome Presence

Our discussion of the work of angels among believers would not be complete without at least a passing recognition of the *awesomeness* of angelic appearances. In

Scripture, believers who were visited by angels frequently responded with great fear during the first few moments. I make this point not because we *should* fear angels. (Obviously, we're not to fear angels; we're to praise God that He has made these glorious provisions for our well-being.) Rather, I bring this up because many of the bestselling angel enthusiasts today are teaching that angel appearances are nonthreatening and easy to take.

According to current literature, angel appearances can allegedly take the form of nudgings, intuition, or coincidence.[24] They can appear as light on the water, or in clouds and rainbows.[25] They can even appear as a swan.[26] In fact, we are told that angel appearances can "take whatever form the visited person is *willing to accept.*"[27]

Contrary to this, the Bible gives no indication whatsoever that angels appear to humans according to whatever form they are willing to accept. Rather, the visitation of angels typically involves a glorious and awesome appearance that brings fear and trembling to a person.

For example, when Daniel saw an angel he was left without strength (Daniel 10:8).[28] Zechariah was gripped with fear when an angel appeared to him while he was in the Temple (Luke 1:12). The shepherds in the field were very much afraid when an angel appeared to them (Luke 2:9). The Roman soldiers trembled with fear and became as dead men when an angel appeared and rolled back the stone blocking Jesus' tomb (Matthew 28:2-4).

My point, then, is that angelic appearances to believers in biblical times were so awesome and so glorious that it was natural to respond with fear. God's holy angels are magnificent and beautiful beings, and their overwhelming appearance is something that man is not accustomed to.

. . . . .

Now, despite the awesome and glorious appearance of angels, Scripture is consistent in emphasizing that we are *never* to worship them. As we noted earlier, the apostle Paul explicitly condemns the worship of angels in Colossians 2:18. The angels themselves refuse worship and affirm that God alone is worthy of such honor (Revelation 19:10; 22:8-9). God Himself explicitly commands that *only He* is to be worshiped (Exodus 20:5-6).

Rejoicing in God's Provision

In this chapter we have sought to attain a balanced and biblical understanding of the work angels have among we who are believers. We've looked not only at the various ministries of angels among us, but we've also looked at the proper attitude we are to have toward them.

Perhaps theologian Charles Hodge sums it up best with these words:

> This Scriptural doctrine of the ministry of angels is full of consolation for the people of God. They may rejoice in the assurance that these holy beings encamp round about them, defending them day and night from unseen enemies and unapprehended dangers. At the same time they must not come between us and God. We are not to look to them nor to invoke their aid. They are in the hands of God and exercise His will.[29]

The work of angels among believers is truly an exciting doctrine, for it points to God's great concern for us. Billy Graham therefore exhorts us, "Believers, look up—take courage. The angels are nearer than you think."[30] Amen!

. . . . .

Then I heard a loud voice from the temple saying to the seven angels, "Go, pour out the seven bowls of God's wrath on the earth."

—Revelation 16:1

·13·

*Angels Among **Them***

Many angel enthusiasts today say that interacting with angels is a way of being spiritual without having to involve God. Bestselling angel author Sophy Burnham suggests that the current popularity of angels is "because we have created this concept of God as punitive, jealous, judgmental." She assures us that "angels never are. They are utterly compassionate."[1]

Regardless of what form an angelic appearance may take, we are told, the messages from angels are always very positive. Indeed, Burnham says the typical message from an angel is, "Don't be afraid, everything is just fine. There is nothing but love."[2] Things are going to work out, the angels consistently communicate.[3]

We are also told that one way to tell whether we have encountered an angel has to do with the aftereffects of angelic visitations. Burnham, for example, says that a common mark of an angelic visitation is that it "brings a calm and peaceful serenity that descends sweetly over you, and this is true even when the angel is not seen."[4]

Alma Daniel, Timothy Wyllie, and Andrew Ramer, authors of *Ask Your Angels*, agree, suggesting that "feelings of love, of greater self-acceptance, of inner peace, of being deeply cared for and recognized, are signs of angelic connection."[5] Even if we don't see anything tangible, angelic presence can be detected via the above characteristics.

From reading the current literature, it would seem that angels have nothing but good news and happiness for the world of human beings. However, this is not the picture portrayed of angels in the Scriptures. Certainly we read of the great benefit of angelic involvement in the lives of believers, but for those who *reject* the Christ of the Bible, it is a wholly different story.

Promoting Evangelism

In the New Testament there is at least one occasion in which an angel guides an evangelist (Philip) to a sinner (an Ethiopian treasurer) (Acts 8:26). There is another case in which an angel guides a sinner (Cornelius) to an evangelist (Peter) (Acts 10:1-8).[6] In both incidents, angels were used by God to assist in the work of evangelism.[7]

Such angelic involvement in evangelistic activity may not be a normative, everyday occurrence for Christians. But given the need and the circumstances, it is possible that even today God may choose on occasion to providentially utilize His holy angels in bringing sinners and evangelists together.

What we learn from this is that God loves sinners so much that, when conditions warrant it, He is willing to go to extreme means to reach people with the message of the Gospel. This puts an exclamation point on what we read in 2 Peter 3:9, which says that God does not want *anyone* to perish.

. . . . .

Restraining Wickedness

There are at least a few occasions in Scripture where we find God's holy angels involved in the work of restraining evil. For example, in the book of Genesis we read about some angels who struck a group of wicked men with blindness so the men couldn't carry out their evil intentions when they came to Lot's house (Genesis 18:22; 19:1,10-11).[8] The angels then helped Lot and his family escape from Sodom prior to the judgment that fell on that wicked city (19:14-15).

Is it possible that God's angels have acted in the past to restrain some evil from befalling you? I'd say *absolutely!* I think back to the true story I shared in chapter 1 regarding the missionary John Paton and his wife, who lived on the New Hebrides Islands. Hostile natives were set to attack the missionary headquarters one night, but the Patons prayed to God and the natives suddenly turned away and left. Paton later found out that the tribe had refrained from attacking because they saw that the headquarters was surrounded by hundreds of "men," all dressed in shining garments with swords drawn.[9]

When we get to heaven and fellowship face to face with God's holy angels, perhaps we will discover that there were many occasions in which the angels acted to restrain some evil from befalling us in the course of our day-to-day affairs. We should be thankful to God for this angelic ministry.

Announcing Judgments

We noted earlier that some angels helped Lot and his family escape from Sodom before the city was destroyed. This sobering event is a great example of how angels are used by God to announce impending judgments. On this occasion the angels said to Lot, "We are going to destroy this place. The outcry to the LORD against its people is so great that he has sent us to destroy it" (Genesis 19:13).

In the book of Revelation we see that God's angels will announce judgments throughout the future seven-year Tribulation period (which will follow the Rapture of the church). For example, in Revelation 14—prior to the outpouring of God's seven "bowl judgments" on the earth—we read that an angel will fly through the air proclaiming with a loud voice, "Fear God and give him glory, because the hour of his judgment has come. Worship him who made the heavens, the earth, the sea and the springs of water" (verse 7).

Another angel will follow and announce,

> If anyone worships the beast and his image and receives his mark on the forehead or on the hand, he, too, will drink of the wine of God's fury, which has been poured full strength into the cup of his wrath. He will be tormented with burning sulfur in the presence of the holy angels and of the Lamb (verses 8-10).

At the very end of the Tribulation period, the angels will make still another announcement of judgment. The apostle John describes this for us:

> I saw an angel standing in the sun, who cried in a loud voice to all the birds flying in midair, "Come, gather together for the great supper of God, so that you may eat the flesh of kings, generals, and mighty men, of horses and their riders, and the flesh of all people, free and slave, small and great" (Revelation 19:17-18).

What can we deduce from all this? For one thing, the New Age angel enthusiasts who say that the typical message from an angel is, "Don't be afraid, everything is just fine. There is nothing but love"[10] *are in gross error*. Though angels *are* loving and *do* bring comfort to the people of God, they also bring messages of death, destruction, and judgment to those who reject Christ.

Executing Judgment

Angels not only announce God's impending judgments, they also *execute* them. A prime example of this may be found in Acts 12. Here we read that on a particular day Herod put on his royal robes, sat on his throne, and delivered a public address to the people. His listeners then shouted, "This is the voice of a god, not of a man" (Acts 12:22). Verse 23 tells us what happened next: "Immediately, because Herod did not give praise to God, an angel of the Lord struck him down, and he was eaten by worms and died." Pretenders to the divine throne are not permitted by God. And in this case, an angel of God was given authority to take a human being's life in judgment.

During the Tribulation, God will use His angels to execute many judgments against an unbelieving world. For example, according to Revelation 8, angels are involved in the seven "trumpet judgments" that are poured out on humankind. In these judgments, hail and fire will fall upon the earth, a third of the earth will burn up, the sea will turn into blood, a third of the living creatures in the sea will die, the waters of the earth will become undrinkable, and much more will happen (*see* verses 5-13).

Likewise, we read in Revelation 16:1, "I heard a loud voice from the temple saying to the seven angels, 'Go, pour out the seven bowls of God's wrath on the earth.'" These particular judgments, which will be inflicted by angels, will result in such horrors as painful sores, death, unbearably intense heat from the sun, darkness over the land, and a violent earthquake (*see* verses 2-18). The Tribulation will truly be a frightening time to be living on this planet.

Reaping the Harvest

In His parable of the weeds, Jesus speaks about sowing good seed in a field, pulling up weeds and burning them, and bringing in the harvest. In Matthew 13:37-43, He explains the symbolism of this parable:

> The one who sowed the good seed is the Son of Man. The field is the world, and the good seed stands for the sons of the kingdom. The weeds are the sons of the evil one, and the enemy who sows them is the devil. The harvest is the end of the age, and *the harvesters are angels*. As the weeds are pulled up and burned in the fire, so it will be at the end of the age. The Son of Man will *send out his angels*, and *they* will weed out of his kingdom everything that causes sin and all who do evil. *They* will throw them into the fiery furnace, where there will be weeping and gnashing of teeth (emphasis added).

What this sobering passage tells us is that at the end of the age, God's angels will actually take hold of Christ-rejecting evildoers and "throw them into the fiery furnace." Tragically, modern angel enthusiasts—especially those of the New Age variety—fail to recognize this somber aspect of the work of angels.

No matter how many pleasures Satan offers you, his ultimate intention is to ruin you. Your destruction is his highest priority.

—Erwin W. Lutzer[1]

·14·

Fallen Angels

The biblical evidence for the existence and activity of Satan and demons is formidable. Seven books in the Old Testament specifically teach the reality of Satan (Genesis, 1 Chronicles, Job, Psalms, Isaiah, Ezekiel, and Zechariah). Every New Testament writer and 19 of the books make specific reference to him (for example, Matthew 4:10; 12:26; Mark 1:13; 3:23,26; 4:15; Luke 11:18; 22:3; John 13:27). Jesus Christ refers to Satan some 25 times.

Some people throughout church history have claimed that Satan is not a real person—an idea no doubt inspired by Satan himself. After all, if there is no real "enemy," then certainly there will be no preparation for defense. And if there is no preparation for defense, then the enemy can attack at will and work his evil while remaining incognito.

The Bible is just as certain of Satan's existence as of God's existence. It reveals that Satan is both a fallen angel *and* a genuine person. How do we know he is a person? The Scriptures reveal that Satan has all the attributes of personality—including *mind* (2 Corinthians 11:3), *emo-tions* (Luke 22:31; Revelation 12:17), and *will* (Isaiah 14:12-14; 2 Timothy 2:26). Not only that, but personal pronouns are used to describe him (Job 1; Matthew 4:1-12). As well, Satan performs personal actions (Matthew 4:1-11; John 8:44; 1 John 3:8; Jude 9).

The Scriptures portray Satan as a created being who—though powerful—has definite limitations. Satan does not possess attributes that belong to God alone, such as *omnipresence* (being everywhere-present), *omnipotence* (being all-powerful), and *omniscience* (being all-knowing). Satan is a *creature*, and as such he is lesser than (and is responsible to) the Creator. Satan can only be in one place at one time; his strength (though great) is limited; and his knowledge (though great) is limited.

Even though Satan possesses creaturely limitations, he is nevertheless pictured in Scripture as being extremely powerful and influential in the world. He is called the "ruler of this world" (John 12:31 NASB), "the god of this world" (2 Corinthians 4:4 KJV) and the "prince of the power of the air" (Ephesians 2:2 KJV). He is also said to deceive the whole world (Revelation 12:9: 20:3). He is portrayed as having power in the governmental realm (Matthew 4:8-9; 2 Corinthians 4:4), the physical realm (Luke 13:11,16; Acts 10:38), the angelic realm (Ephesians 6:11-12; Jude 9), and the ecclesiastical (church) realm (Revelation 2:9; 3:9). Clearly, Christians should be very concerned about Satan.

A key question we want to address in this chapter is, *Where* did Satan and the demons come from? Did God create Satan and demons as evil beings, or were they holy at one time? These are critical questions that demand good answers.

Evidence for Lucifer's Fall

Many Bible scholars down through the centuries have believed that a description of Lucifer's fall is found in Ezekiel 28 and Isaiah 14. Let us briefly consider these passages.

Ezekiel 28:11-19—Pride and Judgment

It appears from the context of Ezekiel 28 that the first ten verses of this chapter are dealing with a human leader. Then, starting in verse 11 and on through verse 19, Lucifer is the focus of discussion.[2] Let us briefly consider these latter verses:

> The word of the LORD came to me: "Son of man, take up a lament concerning the king of Tyre and say to him: 'This is what the Sovereign LORD says:
>
> "'You were the *model of perfection, full of wisdom* and *perfect in beauty.*
>
> *You were in Eden,* the *garden of God;* every precious stone adorned you: ruby, topaz and emerald, chrysolite, onyx and jasper, sapphire, turquoise and beryl.
>
> Your settings and mountings were made of gold; on the day you were created they were prepared.
>
> You were anointed as a *guardian cherub,* for so I ordained you.
>
> *You were on the holy mount of God;* you walked among the fiery stones.
>
> You were *blameless in your ways* from the day you were created till wickedness was found in you.
>
> Through your widespread trade you were filled with violence, and you sinned.

So *I drove you in disgrace from the mount of God*, and I
expelled you, O *guardian cherub*, from among the
fiery stones.
Your heart became proud on account of your beauty, and
you *corrupted your wisdom because of your splendor*.
So *I threw you to the earth*; I made a spectacle of you
before kings.
By your many sins and dishonest trade you have
desecrated your sanctuaries.
So I made a fire come out from you, and it con-
sumed you, and I reduced you to ashes on the
ground in the sight of all who were watching.
All the nations who knew you are appalled at you;
you have come to a horrible end and will be no
more'" (emphasis added).

What is the rationale for the conclusion that these
verses refer to the fall of Lucifer? Notice that after the
first ten verses in this chapter speak about the *ruler* of
Tyre (who was condemned for claiming to be a god
though he was just a man), the discussion then moves to
the *king* of Tyre starting in verse 11. The switch from
"ruler" to "king" and the allusions to the Garden of Eden
seem to imply that the individual described here was
more than human.[3] Many scholars believe that though
there was a human "ruler" of Tyre, the *real* "king" of Tyre
was Satan, for it was he who was ultimately at work in
this wicked, anti-God city and it was he who worked
through the human ruler of the city.

Some people have suggested that these verses may
actually be dealing with a human king of Tyre who was
empowered by Satan. Charles Ryrie, for example, suggests that "the historic king of Tyre was simply a tool of
Satan, possibly indwelt by him. And in describing this
king, Ezekiel also gives us glimpses of the superhuman
creature, Satan, who was using, if not indwelling, him."[4]

. . . . .

Thomas Ice and Robert Dean, in their book *Overrun by Demons*, note that in Scripture Satan is sometimes "addressed through the creature he is influencing. For example, when Jesus foretold His crucifixion, Peter began to rebuke Him. But Jesus rebuked Peter and said, 'Get behind Me, Satan!' (Matthew 16:23). In addition, when God pronounced a curse on Satan in Genesis 3:14-15 He addressed Satan indirectly through the serpent."[5] Hence, even though a "king" is spoken about in Ezekiel 28:11-19, the ultimate subject of these verses may be Satan.

Note also that there are things that are true of this "king" that—at least ultimately—cannot be said to be true of human beings.[6] For example, the king is portrayed as having a *different nature* than man (he is a cherub, considered to be in the "inner circle" of angels with closest access to God, Ezekiel 28:14); he had a *different position* than man (he was blameless and sinless, verse 15); he was in a *different realm* than man (the holy mount of God, verses 13-14; cf. Genesis 3:1-7); he received a *different judgment* than man (he was cast out of the mountain of God and thrown to the earth [verse 16], which seems to parallel the description of Satan's fall in Revelation 12); and the superlatives used to describe him don't seem to fit that of a human being ("full of wisdom," "perfect in beauty," and having "the model of perfection," verse 12).

Our text tells us that this king was a created being and left the creative hand of God in a perfect state (Ezekiel 28:12,15). "God did not create Satan as some prime minister of evil. As with all God's Creation, Satan was a perfectly created being—one of the crowning achievements in God's angelic realm."[7]

One theologian has suggested that Lucifer "awoke in the first moment of his existence in the full-orbed

. . . . .

beauty and power of his exalted position; surrounded by all the magnificence which God gave him. He saw himself as above all the hosts in power, wisdom, and beauty. Only at the throne of God itself did he see more than he himself possessed. . . . Before his fall he may be said to have occupied the role of prime minister for God, ruling possibly over the universe but certainly over this world."[8]

Ezekiel 28 tells us that this "king" was perfect in his ways until iniquity was found in him (verse 15). What was this iniquity? We read in verse 17, "Your heart became proud on account of your beauty, and you corrupted your wisdom because of your splendor." Lucifer apparently became so impressed with his own beauty, brilliance, intelligence, power, and position that he began to desire for himself the honor and glory that belonged to God alone. The sin that corrupted Lucifer was self-generated pride.

Apparently, this represents the actual beginning of sin in the universe—preceding the fall of the human Adam by an indeterminate time. Sin originated in the free will of Lucifer, who—with full understanding of the issues involved—chose to rebel against the Creator.

This mighty angelic being was rightfully judged by God: "I threw you to the earth" (Ezekiel 28:17). This doesn't mean that Satan had no further access to heaven, for other scriptures clearly indicate that Satan maintained this access even after his fall (for example, Job 1:6-12; Zechariah 3:1-2). However, Ezekiel 28:17 indicates that Satan was completely cast out of God's heavenly government and his place of authority (cf. Luke 10:18).

One final evidence: It is interesting to note that all that is said of this "king of Tyre" in Ezekiel 28 is elsewhere stated in Scripture of the person of Lucifer or Satan.

Isaiah 14:12-17—Pretender to the Divine Throne

Isaiah 14:12-17 is another Old Testament passage that many scholars believe refers to the fall of Lucifer:

> How you have fallen from heaven, O morning star, son of the dawn!
>
> You have been cast down to the earth, you who once laid low the nations!
>
> You said in your heart, *"I will ascend to heaven; I will raise my throne above the stars of God; I will sit enthroned on the mount of assembly, on the utmost heights of the sacred mountain. I will ascend above the tops of the clouds; I will make myself like the Most High."*
>
> But you are brought down to the grave, to the depths of the pit.
>
> Those who see you stare at you, they ponder your fate: "Is this the man who shook the earth and made kingdoms tremble, the man who made the world a desert, who overthrew its cities and would not let his captives go home?" (emphasis added).

Now, some Bible scholars see no reference whatsoever to Lucifer in this passage.[9] They argue that the being mentioned in this verse is referred to *as a man* (Isaiah 14:16) and is compared with other kings on the earth (verse 18). And the statement, "How you have fallen from heaven" (verse 12) is alleged to refer to a fall from great political heights.[10]

There are other scholars who interpret this passage as referring *only* to the fall of Lucifer, with no reference whatsoever to a human king. The argument here is that the description of this being is beyond humanness, and hence could not refer to a mere mortal man.

. . . . .

There is a third view that I think is preferable to the two views above. This view sees Isaiah 14:12-17 as having a *dual* reference. It may be that verses 4 through 11 deal with an actual king of Babylon. Then, in verses 12 through 17, we find a dual reference that includes not just the king of Babylon but a typological description of Lucifer as well.

If Isaiah 14 does indeed contain a reference to the fall of Lucifer, then the pattern of this passage would seem to fit that of the Ezekiel 28 reference—that is, first a human leader is described, and then dual reference is made to a human leader *and* Satan.

It is significant that the language used to describe this being fits other passages in the Bible that speak about Satan. For example, the five "I wills" in Isaiah 14 indicate an element of pride, which was also evidenced in Ezekiel 28:17 (cf. 1 Timothy 3:6, which makes reference to Satan's conceit). Let's examine this pride in more detail by looking at the five "I wills" in Isaiah 14:13-14 and considering how each may indicate something about Lucifer's fall:

"I will ascend to heaven." Apparently Lucifer wanted to abide in heaven and desired equal recognition alongside God Himself.

"I will raise my throne above the stars of God." The "stars" likely have reference to the angels of God. Lucifer apparently desired to rule over the angelic realm with the same authority as God.

"I will sit enthroned on the mount of assembly, on the utmost heights of the sacred mountain." Scripture elsewhere indicates that the "mount of assembly" is a reference to the center of God's kingdom rule (*see* Isaiah 2:2; Psalm 48:2). The phrase is sometimes associated with the Messiah's future earthly rule in Jerusalem during the millennial kingdom. Hence, it may be that Satan desired to rule over humans in place of the Messiah.[11]

. . . . .

"I will ascend above the tops of the clouds." In the Bible, clouds often metaphorically represent the glory of God (Exodus 13:21; 40:28-34; Matthew 26:64; Revelation 14:14). Apparently Lucifer sought a glory equal to that of God Himself.

"I will make myself like the Most High." Scripture describes God as the possessor of heaven and earth (Genesis 14:18-19). Apparently Lucifer sought the supreme position of the universe for Himself. "Satan wanted to be as powerful as God. He wanted to exercise the authority and control in this world that rightfully belongs only to God. His sin was a direct challenge to the power and authority of God."[12]

If Isaiah 14:12-17 is a reference to the fall of Lucifer, as I believe it is, then I want to emphasize that Lucifer's sin against God is especially vile and wicked for a number of reasons. First, there was no previous example of sin in the universe. Lucifer was the first to fall. Second, Lucifer was originally created by God in a state of beauty and perfection. He had everything going for him, but he corrupted himself. Third, Lucifer had incredibly great intelligence—and was certainly aware that there would be consequences for rebelling against the Creator. And fourth, Lucifer enjoyed perfect fellowship with the Creator.[13] Despite living in such a perfect environment, however, Lucifer still rebelled against the One who brought him into being.

Satan's sin, of course, had widespread effects. "It affected other angels (Revelation 12:7); it affects all people (Ephesians 2:2); it positioned him as the ruler of this world (John 16:11); it affects all the nations of the world, for he works to deceive them (Revelation 20:3)."[14] Satan's act of rebellion was one of unfathomable consequences.

As a result of this heinous sin against God, Lucifer was banished from living in heaven (Isaiah 14:12). He

. . . . .

became corrupt, and his name changed from *Lucifer* ("morning star") to *Satan* ("adversary"). His power became completely perverted (Isaiah 14:12,16,17). Following the second coming of Christ, he will be bound in a pit during the 1,000-year millennial kingdom over which Christ will rule (Revelation 20:3). And eventually, he will be thrown into the lake of fire (Matthew 25:41).

Now, a key question that has fascinated Bible students throughout the centuries has to do with *when* Lucifer fell. Scripture does not pinpoint for us when this horrendous event occurred. However, it had to be before the events described in Genesis 3 (the temptation of Adam and Eve) because Satan (formerly Lucifer) took part in that temptation (2 Corinthians 11:3). So, the most we can say is that Lucifer's fall took place sometime prior to the fall of Adam and Eve.

How Scripture Describes Satan

It is fascinating to study the various ways the Bible speaks about Satan. Indeed, we learn much about him and his work by the various names and titles used of him. For example:

• Satan is called the *accuser of the brethren* (Revelation 12:10). The Greek text of this verse indicates that accusing God's people is a continuous, ongoing work of Satan. He never lets up; he accuses God's people "day and night." Thomas Ice and Robert Dean note that "Satan opposes God's people in two ways. First, he brings charges against believers before God (Zechariah 3:1; Romans 8:33). Second, he accuses believers to their own conscience."[15]

• Satan is called our *adversary* (1 Peter 5:8 KJV). This word indicates that Satan opposes us and stands against us in every way he can.

. . . . .

• Satan is called *Beelzebub* (Matthew 12:24). This word literally means "lord of the flies," carrying the idea "lord of filth." The Devil corrupts everything he touches.

• Satan is called the *Devil* (Matthew 4:1). This word carries the idea of "adversary" as well as "slanderer." Satan was and is the adversary of Christ; he is the adversary of all who follow Christ. He slanders God to man (Genesis 3:1-7), and man to God (Job 1:9; 2:4). Keep in mind that a slanderer is someone who utters malicious false reports that injure the reputation of another.[16]

• Satan is called our *enemy* (Matthew 13:39). This term comes from a root word meaning "hatred." It characterizes Satan's attitude in an absolute sense. He hates both God and His children.

• Satan is called the *evil one* (1 John 5:19). He is "the opposer of all that is good and the promoter of all that is evil."[17] Indeed, he is the very embodiment of evil.

• Satan is called the *father of lies* (John 8:44). The word "father" is used here metaphorically of the originator of a family or company of persons animated by a deceitful character. Satan was the first and greatest liar.

• Satan is called a *murderer* (John 8:44). This word literally means "man killer" (cf. 1 John 3:12,15). Hatred is the motive that leads a person to commit murder. Satan hates both God and His children, so he has a genuine motive for murder. Ray Stedman notes that "because he is a liar and a murderer, the Devil's work is to deceive and to destroy. There you have the explanation for all that has been going on in human history throughout the whole course of the record of man . . . . Whom the Devil cannot deceive, he tries to destroy, and whom he cannot destroy, he attempts to deceive."[18]

• Satan is called the *god of this age* (2 Corinthians 4:4). Of course, this does not mean that Satan is deity. It simply means this is an evil age, and Satan is its "god" in

. . . . .

the sense that he is the head of it. Also, as "god of this age," Satan is in "back of the false cults and systems that have cursed the true church through the ages."[19]

• Satan is called the *prince of the power of the air* (Ephesians 2:2 KJV). It appears that the "air" in this context is that sphere in which the inhabitants of this world live. This sphere represents the very seat of Satan's authority.

• Satan is called the *prince of this world* (John 12:31; 14:30; 16:11). The key term here is "world." This word refers not to the physical earth but to "a vast order or system that Satan has promoted which conforms to his ideals, aims, and methods."[20]

• Satan is called a *roaring lion* (1 Peter 5:8-9). This graphic simile depicts Satan's strength and destructiveness.

• Satan is called the *tempter* (Matthew 4:3). "This name indicates his constant purpose and endeavor to incite man to sin. He presents the most plausible excuses and suggests the most striking advantages for sinning."[21]

• Satan is called a *serpent* (Genesis 3:1; Revelation 12:9). This word symbolizes the origin of sin in the Garden of Eden as well as the hatefulness and deadly effect of sin. The serpent is characterized by treachery, deceitfulness, venom, and murderous proclivities.

This brief survey of names and titles makes it clear that Satan's avowed purpose is to thwart the plan of God in every area he can and by every means possible. Toward this end, Satan promotes a world system of which he is the ruler and which stands in full opposition to God.

Satan's Vast Experience

It is critical that Christians realize that Satan has vast experience in bringing people down. In fact, his experience is far greater than any person's has ever been. As Charles Ryrie says,

> By his very longevity Satan has acquired a breadth and depth of experience which he matches against the limited knowledge of man. He has observed other believers in every conceivable situation, thus enabling him to predict with accuracy how we will respond to circumstances. Although Satan is not omniscient, his wide experience and observation of man throughout his entire history on earth give him knowledge which is far superior to anything any man could have.[22]

Because of his vast experience, Satan knows what will likely work in his attempt to foul you up. He is a master tempter who, for thousands of years, has successfully lured humans into sin. *Christian beware!*

Satan as "the Ape of God"

It was Augustine who called the Devil *Simius Dei*—"the ape of God." Satan is the great counterfeiter.[23] He mimics God in many ways. "The principal tactic Satan uses to attack God and His program in general is to offer a counterfeit kingdom and program."[24] This is hinted at in 2 Corinthians 11:14, which makes reference to Satan *masquerading* as an "angel of light."

In what ways does Satan act as "the ape of God"? Consider the following:

• Satan has his own *church*—the "synagogue of Satan" (Revelation 2:9).

• Satan has his own *ministers*—ministers of darkness who bring false sermons (2 Corinthians 11:4-5).

• Satan has formulated his own *system of theology*—called "doctrines of demons" (1 Timothy 4:1 NASB; *see also* Revelation 2:24).

• His ministers proclaim his *gospel*—"a gospel other than the one we preached to you" (Galatians 1:7-8).

• Satan has his own *throne* (Revelation 13:2) and his own *worshipers* (13:4).

• Satan inspires *false Christs* and self-constituted messiahs (Matthew 24:4-5).

• Satan employs *false teachers* who bring in "destructive heresies" (2 Peter 2:1).

• Satan sends out *false prophets* (Matthew 24:11).

• Satan sponsors *false apostles* who imitate the true (2 Corinthians 11:13).

In view of such mimicking, one theologian has concluded that "Satan's plan and purposes have been, are, and always will be to seek to establish a rival rule to God's kingdom. He is promoting a system of which he is the head and which stands in opposition to God and His rule in the universe."[25]

Satan's Attempts to Thwart Christ

As we trace the history of the New Testament it becomes clear that Satan had a dark agenda in trying to thwart the person and mission of Jesus Christ. Consider the following historical facts:

• According to Matthew 2, Joseph, Mary, and Jesus had to flee to Egypt—having been warned by an angel—because Herod ordered the slaughter of all male children, hoping to kill Christ in the process (verses 13-16). Now, the account in Matthew does not mention the involvement of Satan, but it was nevertheless a satanic act. Revelation 12:4-6 appears to support the idea that Satan sought Jesus' death shortly after His birth.

. . . . .

• Following His baptism, Jesus was led into the wilderness, where He was tempted by the Devil for 40 days (Matthew 4:1-11). Of course, Christ *as God* could not be made to sin. But Satan still made the attempt in hopes of disqualifying Christ from being the Savior.

• During some of His encounters with Israel's religious leaders, Jesus saw the work of Satan in their actions. For example, some of the Jewish leaders sought to have Jesus put to death. So Jesus responded, "You belong to your father, the devil, and you want to carry out your father's desire. *He was a murderer from the beginning*" (John 8:44, emphasis added).

• Jesus also saw the work of Satan among those He was closest to. For example, when Jesus predicted His own death, Peter rebuked Him and said, "Never, Lord! . . . This shall never happen to you!" (Matthew 16:22). Jesus then said to Peter, "Get behind Me, Satan!" (verse 23 NASB). Jesus recognized, in Peter's words, Satan's attempt to stop Him from going to the cross.

These and other verses indicate that the Devil did everything he could to thwart the mission of Jesus Christ. The spiritual warfare must have been brutal; there is no way for us to know *just how much* spiritual warfare our Lord must have encountered on the road to Calvary.

The Six Judgments of Satan

Within the pages of Scripture we find that there are six distinct judgments against Satan:

• Following his initial rebellion against God, he was cast from his original position of privilege in heaven (Ezekiel 28:16).

• He was judged in the Garden of Eden following his role in leading Adam and Eve into sin (Genesis 3:14-15).

. . . . .

• He was judged at the cross (John 12:31; cf. Colossians 2:15; Hebrews 2:14).[26] "Christ partook of humanity, and through His substitutionary death He defeated Satan, rendering him impotent in the believer's life."[27]

• He will be cast out of heaven in the middle of the seven-year Tribulation period (Revelation 12:13). During this time he will be barred from all access to heaven.

• He will be confined in "the Abyss" during the future 1,000-year millennial kingdom over which Christ will rule (Revelation 20:2).

• He will be cast into the lake of fire at the end of the millennial kingdom, where he will dwell for the rest of eternity (Revelation 20:10; cf. Matthew 25:41).

What we learn from the above passages is that even though Satan is presently active in our world, he is a judged being and is destined for eternal suffering. While the execution of these judgments is not yet complete, the judgments have been pronounced and it's just a matter of time before Satan's final doom is brought about.

The World of Demons

What about the demons (or "hell's angels")? Where did they come from? Are there any references in the Bible to the fall of numerous angels who became demons? I believe there are some hints in Scripture that help us answer these questions.

Many scholars believe the first five verses of Revelation 12 contain a minihistory of Satan. In keeping with this, it would seem Revelation 12:4 refers to the fall of the angels who followed Satan: "His [Satan's] tail swept a third of the stars out of the sky and flung them to the earth."[28] It has long been recognized that in the Bible, the word "stars" is sometimes used of angels (*see* Job 38:7). If "stars" refers to angels in Revelation 12:4, it would appear that after Lucifer rebelled against God, he was able to draw a third of the angelic realm after him. When he sinned, he did not sin alone, but apparently led a massive angelic revolt against God.

Just a few verses later, we read of the "dragon *and his angels*" (Revelation 12:7, emphasis added; cf. Ephesians 3:10; 6:12). There is little doubt that demons are simply fallen angels.[29] Elsewhere in the Bible, Satan (himself a fallen angel) is called "the prince of demons" (Matthew 12:24). Demons are Satan's emissaries; they promote his purpose to thwart the plan of God.

The demons are highly committed to their dark prince, Satan:

> These spirits, having [made] an irrevocable choice to follow Satan, instead of remaining loyal to their Creator, have become irretrievably confirmed in wickedness, and irreparably abandoned to delusion. Hence, they are in full sympathy with their prince, and render him willing service in their varied ranks and positions of service in his highly organized kingdom of evil.[30]

Demons are portrayed in Scripture as being evil and wicked. They are designated "unclean spirits" (Matthew 10:1 KJV), "evil spirits" (Luke 7:21), and "spiritual forces of evil" (Ephesians 6:12). All these terms point to the immoral nature of demons. It is not surprising, then, that many people involved in the occult are also involved in immorality.[31]

What kinds of wicked things do demons do? Among many other things, Scripture says they inflict physical diseases on people (such as speechlessness, Matthew 9:33; blindness, 12:22; and epilepsy, 17:15-18). They also afflict people with mental disorders (Mark 5:4-5; 9:20-22;

. . . . .

Luke 8:27-29; 9:37-42). They cause people to be self-destructive (Mark 5:5; Luke 9:42). They are even responsible for the deaths of some people (Revelation 9:14-19).

Of course, we must be careful to note that even though demons can cause physical illnesses, Scripture distinguishes natural illnesses from those that are demon-caused (Matthew 4:24; Mark 1:32; Luke 7:21; 9:1; Acts 5:16). Theologian Millard J. Erickson notes that "in the case of numerous healings no mention is made of demons. In Matthew, for example, no mention is made of demon exorcism in the case of the healing of the centurion's servant (8:5-13), the woman with the hemorrhage of twelve years' duration (9:19-20), the two blind men (9:27-30), the man with the withered hand (12:9-14), and those who touched the fringe of Jesus' garment (14:35-36)."[32] Hence, you must not presume you are being afflicted by a demon every time you get sick.

Presently there are two classes or groups of demons: One group is free and active in opposing God and His people (Ephesians 2:1-3); the other group is confined. Charles Ryrie notes that "of those who are confined, some are temporarily so, while others are permanently confined in Tartarus (2 Peter 2:4 and Jude 6). The Greeks thought of Tartarus as a place of punishment lower than hades. Those temporarily confined are in the abyss (Luke 8:31; Revelation 9:1-3,11), some apparently consigned there to await final judgment, while others will be loosed to be active on the earth [during the seven-year Tribulation] (verse 1-3,11,14; 16:14)."[33]

Why are some fallen angels permanently confined? It seems reasonable to assume that they are being punished for some sin other than the original rebellion against God. Some theologians believe these angels are guilty of the unnatural sin mentioned in Genesis 6:2-4, and because of the gross depravity of this sin, they are permanently confined to Tartarus.[34]

. . . . .

Ranks Among Fallen Angels

Earlier in the book we saw that the angels are organized according to rank. The same is true among the fallen angels (Ephesians 6:12). Their ranks include principalities, powers, rulers of the darkness of this world, and spiritual wickedness in high places.[35] And *all* fallen angels, regardless of their individual ranks, follow the leadership of their malevolent commander-in-chief—Satan, the prince of demons.

The high degree of organization in the kingdom of darkness may sometimes make it seem like Satan is omniscient or omnipotent. Demons report to Satan from all over the world, thereby extending his own reach and influence. But, as we noted earlier, Satan is neither omniscient nor omnipotent. He is a creature with creaturely limitations.

Varying Degrees of Depravity

It appears from the Scriptures that there are varying degrees of depravity among the fallen angels. Jesus spoke of a demon who left his abode but then returned, bringing with him "seven other spirits *more wicked than [him]self*" (Matthew 12:45, emphasis added). Clearly, then, Jesus indicates that some demons are more evil than others. This would seem to be in line with the teaching that some demons have committed acts so depraved that they are presently imprisoned (2 Peter 2:4).

Fallen Angels and Unbelievers

Second Corinthians 4:4 says that Satan blinds the minds of unbelievers to the truth of the gospel. This passage indicates that Satan inhibits the unbeliever's ability to think or reason properly in regard to spiritual matters.[36] One of the ways Satan does this is by leading people to think that *any* way to heaven is as acceptable as another. In other words, Satan promotes the idea that a person doesn't need to believe in Jesus Christ as the *only* means to salvation.

Satan also seeks to snatch the Word of God from the hearts of unbelievers when they hear it (Luke 8:12). Demons, under Satan's lead, seek to disperse false doctrine (1 Timothy 4:1). As well, they wield influence over false prophets (1 John 4:1-4) and seek to turn men to the worship of idols (*see* Leviticus 17:7; Deuteronomy 32:17; Psalm 106:36-38). In short, fallen angels do all they can to spread spiritual deception.

Fallen Angels and Believers

Fallen angels actively seek to harm believers in various ways. For example:

• Satan tempts believers to sin (Ephesians 2:1-3; 1 Thessalonians 3:5).

• Satan tempts believers to lie (Acts 5:3).

• Satan tempts believers to commit sexually immoral acts (1 Corinthians 7:5).

• Satan accuses and slanders believers (Revelation 12:10).

• Satan hinders the work of believers in any way he can (1 Thessalonians 2:18).

• Satan and his demons seek to wage war against and defeat believers (Ephesians 6:11-12).

• Satan sows tares among believers (Matthew 13:38-39).

• Satan incites persecutions against believers (Revelation 2:10).

• Demons hinder answers to the prayers of believers (Daniel 10:12-20).

• Satan is said to oppose Christians with the ferociousness of a hungry lion (1 Peter 5:8).

• Satan plants doubt in the minds of believers (Genesis 3:1-5).

• Satan seeks to foster spiritual pride in the hearts of Christians (1 Timothy 3:6).

• Satan attempts to lead believers away from "the simplicity and purity of devotion to Christ" (2 Corinthians 11:3 NASB).

• Demons endeavor to instigate jealousy and faction among believers (James 3:13-16).

• Demons would separate the believer from Christ if they could (Romans 8:38-39).

• Demons cooperate with Satan in working against believers (Matthew 25:41; Ephesians 6:12; Revelation 12:7-12).

What about Demon Possession?

Theologian Charles Ryrie defines demon possession this way:

> A demon residing in a person, exerting direct control and influence over that person, with certain derangement of mind and/or body. Demon possession is to be distinguished from demon influence or demon activity in relation to a person. The work of the demon in the latter is from the outside; in demon possession it is from within.[37]

A person who is demon-possessed may manifest unusual, superhuman strength (Mark 5:2-4). He may act in bizarre ways such as going nude and living among tombs rather than in a house (Luke 8:27). The possessed person often engages in self-destructive behavior (Matthew 17:15; Mark 5:5).[38] These are just a few of the biblical signs of demon possession.

Ryrie says that according to the definition given above, a Christian cannot be possessed by a demon since he is indwelt by the Holy Spirit.[39] I believe Ryrie is right. Because the Holy Spirit perpetually indwells Christians (1 Corinthians 6:19), they cannot be demon-possessed. I like the way Walter Martin put it: He said that when the Devil knocks on the door of the Christian's heart, the Holy Spirit opens it and says, "Get lost!"

It is noteworthy that in the Scriptures, there is not a single instance of a Christian being said to be demon-possessed. For sure, there are examples of Christians being *afflicted* by the Devil—but not *possessed* by him.

God's Word clearly states that Christians have been delivered from Satan's domain. As Colossians 1:13 says, "He has rescued us from the dominion of darkness and brought us into the kingdom of the Son he loves." In addition, we must remember that "the one who is in you is greater than the one who is in the world" (1 John 4:4). This statement would not make much sense if Christians could be possessed by the Devil.

Having said this, however, we must acknowledge that even though a Christian cannot be possessed, he can still be *oppressed* or *influenced* by demonic powers. But the oppression or influence is *external* to the Christian, not internal. The demons seek to work from outside the Christian to hinder him; they do not work from within him.[40]

The Christian's Defense

We as Christians should be thankful that God has made provision for our defense against Satan and his fallen angels. What does this defense consist of?

. . . . .

• To begin, we must ever keep in mind that twice in the New Testament we are told that the Lord Jesus lives in heaven to make intercession for us (Romans 8:34; Hebrews 7:25). In other words, Jesus prays for us on a regular basis. Certainly His intercession for us includes the kind of intercession He made for His disciples in John 17:15, where He asked the Father to keep them safe from the evil one.

• Beyond this, God has provided us with spiritual armor for our defense (Ephesians 6:11-18). Each piece of armor is important and serves its own special purpose. But you and I must choose to *put on* this armor. God doesn't force us to dress in it. *We do it by choice.* Read Paul's description of this armor:

> Put on the *full armor* of God so that you can take your stand against the devil's schemes.
>
> For our struggle is not against flesh and blood, but against the rulers, against the authorities, against the powers of this dark world and against the spiritual forces of evil in the heavenly realms.
>
> Therefore put on the *full armor* of God, so that when the day of evil comes, you may be able to stand your ground, and after you have done everything, to stand.
>
> Stand firm then, with the *belt of truth* buckled around your waist, with the *breastplate of righteousness* in place, and with your *feet* fitted with the readiness that comes from the gospel of peace.
>
> In addition to all this, take up the *shield of faith*, with which you can extinguish all the flaming arrows of the evil one.
>
> Take the *helmet of salvation* and the *sword of the Spirit*, which is the word of God.

. . . . .

> And pray in the Spirit on all occasions with all
> kinds of prayers and requests.
> With this in mind, be alert and always keep on
> praying for all the saints (emphasis added).

Without wearing this spiritual armor, you and I
don't stand a chance against the forces of darkness. But
with the armor on, victory is ours. "Wearing" this armor
means that our lives will be characterized by such things
as righteousness, obedience to the will of God, faith in
God, and an effective use of the Word of God. These are
what spell DEFEAT for the Devil in your life. In effect,
putting on the armor of God amounts to putting on Jesus
Christ—who Himself defeated the Devil (Matthew 4:3-11;
Acts 10:38). (Good books are available that fully explain
how to "put on" this spiritual armor.[41])

• Effective use of the Word of God is especially
important for spiritual victory. Jesus used the Word to
defeat the Devil during His wilderness temptations
(Matthew 4). We must learn to do the same. Related to
this, Ray Stedman says,

> Obviously, the greater exposure there is
> to Scripture the more the Spirit can use this
> mighty sword in our lives. If you never read
> or study your Bible, you are terribly exposed
> to defeat and despair. You have no defense;
> you have nothing to put up against these
> forces that are at work. Therefore, learn to
> read your Bible regularly.[42]

• Scripture specifically instructs us that each believer must be *informed* and thereby *alert* to the attacks of
Satan (1 Peter 5:8). A prerequisite to defeating an enemy
is to know as much as you can about him—including his

tactics. The apostle Paul says, "We are not [to be] ignorant of his schemes" (2 Corinthians 2:11). We find all the
information we need about this enemy and his schemes
in the Word of God.

• We are instructed to take a decisive stand against
Satan. James 4:7 says, "Resist the devil, and he will flee
from you." This is not a one-time resistance. Rather, we
must steadfastly resist the Devil on a day-to-day basis.
And when we do, he will flee from us. Similarly, Ephesians 6:13-14 tells us to "stand firm" against the Devil.
This we can do not in our own strength but in the
strength of Christ. After all, it was Christ who "dis-
armed the rulers and authorities . . . [and] made a public
display of them, having triumphed over them" (Colossians 2:15).

• We must not give place to the Devil by letting "the
sun go down while you are still angry" toward someone
(Ephesians 4:27). Permitting unrighteous anger to dwell
in our heart gives opportunity to the Devil to work in our
lives.

• We are instructed to rely on the indwelling spirit
of God, remembering that "the one who is in you is
greater than the one who is in the world" (1 John 4:4).

• We should pray for ourselves and for each other.
Jesus set an example for us in the Lord's Prayer by teaching us to pray, "Deliver us from the evil one" (Matthew
6:13). This should be a daily prayer. Jesus also set an
example of how to pray for others in His prayer for Peter:
"Simon, Simon, Satan has asked to sift you as wheat. But
I have prayed for you, Simon, *that your faith may not fail*"
(Luke 22:31-32, emphasis added). We should pray for
each other that we will maintain a strong faith in the face
of adversity.

• Of course, the believer should never, never dabble
in the occult, for this gives the Devil opportunity to work
in our lives (Deuteronomy 18:10-11; cf. Romans 16:19).

· · · · ·

• Finally, we must remember that Satan is "on a leash." He cannot go beyond what God will allow him (the book of Job makes this abundantly clear).[43] Thus, we should rest secure in the fact that God is in control of the universe and realize that Satan cannot simply do as he pleases in our lives.

The Key to Victory

By following the aforementioned disciplines, we will have victory over Satan and his host of demons. And remember, above all, that successfully defeating the powers of darkness rests upon not what *you* can do in your own strength but upon what *Christ* has already done. Indeed, you are *more* than a conqueror through Him who loved us (Romans 8:37)!

PART 4

Our Future
with the Angels

. . . .

I thank thee, O Lord,
that thou hast so set eternity
within my heart that no earthly thing
can ever satisfy me wholly.

—John Baillie (1741-1806)[1]

·15·

Anticipating Eternity

The light in which our glorious God dwells is superior to all things visible. In the words of one writer,

> It is something other than the radiance of all suns and stars. It is not to be beheld by earthly eyes; it is "unapproachable" (1 Timothy 6:16), far removed from all things this side (2 Corinthians 12:4). Only the angels in heaven can behold it (Matthew 18:10); only the spirits of the perfected in the eternal light (Matthew 5:8; 1 John 3:2; Revelation 22:4); only the pure and holy, even as He Himself is pure (1 John 3:2,3).[2]

One day, we as Christians will dwell with Christ face to face in His unveiled, glorious presence. When we receive our glorified resurrection bodies, the perishable will have become imperishable and the mortal will have become immortal (1 Corinthians 15:50-53). Whereas in our present bodies we cannot endure in the direct presence of the triune God (His glory is too great), our resurrection bodies will be specially suited to dwelling in His presence.

Scripture tells us that even now, Christ is preparing an eternal, glorious dwelling place for us (John 14:1-3). If the present created universe with its incredible starry host is any indication of what Christ can do (John 1:3; Colossians 1:16; Hebrews 1:2,10), then this eternal dwelling place must be truly astounding.

Of special relevance to our study of angels is the fact that when we enter into glory, we will be able to perceive angels just as clearly as you and I perceive each other here on earth (1 Corinthians 13:12). We will see them just as clearly as they see us. And we will jointly serve our glorious King—Jesus Christ—from eternity to eternity, from age to age forevermore.

Joining the Angels in Song

One day, the voices of the saved will be joined with the voices of the angels in worship and praise to our eternal God. This glorious scene is described in detail in the book of Revelation:

> After this I looked and there before me was a great multitude that no one could count, from every nation, tribe, people and language, standing before the throne and in front of the Lamb.
>
> They were wearing white robes and were holding palm branches in their hands.
>
> And they cried out in a loud voice: "Salvation belongs to our God, who sits on the throne, and to the Lamb."
>
> All the angels were standing around the throne and around the elders and the four living creatures.

. . . . .

They fell down on their faces before the throne and worshiped God, saying: "Amen! Praise and glory and wisdom and thanks and honor and power and strength be to our God for ever and ever. Amen!" (Revelation 7:9-12).

Imagine what this will be like—over 100 million angels and untold millions of the redeemed singing praises to God in unity and harmony. It gives me shivers just to hear a good human choir of a few dozen people sing a great anthem. But to have hundreds of millions of angels and believers singing in unison . . . *incredible!*

Focusing on God Alone

God's provision of angels should bring much consolation to us during our earthly sojourns as we make our way to the heavenly city (Hebrews 11:16). We may rightly rejoice over the fact that God's holy angels encamp around us, defending us day and night from unseen enemies and unapprehended dangers. However, *we must never let angels come between us and God*. We are not to look to the angels for our refuge, nor are we to invoke their aid. *God* is our refuge and we are to invoke *His* aid— and at *His* prerogative, the angels will render assistance as *He* directs.

In Scripture, it is always God who is on center stage and the angels exist *solely to do His bidding*. They are never seen acting independently of God.

As Christians, let us resolve to be perpetually excited at God's provisions for us (including the angels), yet at the same time may our eyes ever remain focused on our beloved Christ. Let us not become distracted so that we turn away from our first love. *Christ is supreme!*

. . . . .

Facing Adversity

Keeping our eyes focused on Christ is especially important when life throws us a punch (John 16:33). You see, if something bad should happen to you (such as a car wreck), you may be tempted to ask, "Where was my angel?" Hope MacDonald gives us the right perspective with these words:

> We must recognize the fact that every person, at one time or another, will face sickness, heartache, suffering, and death. We remember that our faith and trust is not in a visible angel or in some miraculous deliverance, but in God alone. We rest in the knowledge that God may not always be understood, but He can *always* be trusted.[3]

It is well for us to keep in mind that God sometimes uses adversities in our lives to develop our faith muscles and to make us strong, mature believers. And even though God may not always remove us from the midst of adversity, He will always walk with us *through* it (Psalm 23:4).

If the time ever comes when we witness a visible appearance of one of God's glorious angels, it will be all the sweeter simply because we have learned to trust in Christ without depending on such supernatural occurrences. We have learned from experience that *Christ alone is worthy of our confidence.*

Looking Toward Eternity

As we continue to keep Christ supreme in our hearts, we can ponder the greatness of what lies ahead. As Scripture tells us, "No eye has seen, no ear has heard, no mind has conceived what God has prepared for those who love him" (1 Corinthians 2:9).

The apostle John describes our eternal destiny this way:

> I saw a new heaven and a new earth, for the first heaven and the first earth had passed away, and there was no longer any sea.
>
> I saw the Holy City, the new Jerusalem, coming down out of heaven from God, prepared as a bride beautifully dressed for her husband.
>
> And I heard a loud voice from the throne saying, "Now the dwelling of God is with men, and he will live with them. They will be his people, and God himself will be with them and be their God. He will wipe every tear from their eyes. There will be no more death or mourning or crying or pain, for the old order of things has passed away."
>
> He who was seated on the throne said, "I am making everything new!" Then he said, "Write this down, for these words are trustworthy and true" (Revelation 21:1-5).
>
> Amen!

Bibliography

1. Select Christian Books on Angels

Dickason, C. Fred. *Angels, Elect and Evil*. Chicago: Moody Press. 1978.

Gaebelein, A.C. *What the Bible Says about Angels*. Grand Rapids: Baker Book House, 1993.

Graham, Billy. *Angels: God's Secret Agents*. New York: Doubleday & Co., 1975.

MacDonald, Hope. *When Angels Appear*. Grand Rapids: Zondervan Publishing House, 1982.

Northrup, L.W. *Encounters with Angels*. Wheaton, IL: Tyndale House Publishers, 1993.

2. Books by Modern Angel Enthusiasts

Anderson, Joan Wester. *Where Angels Walk*. New York: Ballantine Books, 1992.

Burnham, Sophy. *A Book of Angels*. New York: Ballantine Books, 1990.

_____. *Angel Letters*. New York: Ballantine Books, 1991.

Connolly, David. *In Search of Angels: A Celestial Sourcebook for Beginning Your Journey*. New York: Perigee Books, 1993.

Daniel, Alma; Wyllie, Timothy; and Ramer, Andrew. *Ask Your Angels*. New York: Ballantine Books, 1992.

Freeman, Eileen Elias. *Touched by Angels: True Cases of Close Encounters of the Celestial Kind*. New York: Warner Books, 1993.

Goldman, Karen. *Angel Voices*. New York: Simon & Schuster, 1993.

Howard, Jane M. *Commune with the Angels*. Virginia Beach, VA: A.R.E. Press, 1992.

Price, John Randolph. *The Angels Within Us*. New York: Fawcett Columbine, 1993.

Ronner, John. *Do You Have a Guardian Angel?* Murfreesboro, TN: Mamre Press, 1993.

_____. *Know Your Angels*. Murfreesboro, TN: Mamre Press, 1993.

Smith, Robert C. *In the Presence of Angels*. Virginia Beach, VA: A.R.E. Press, 1993.

Taylor, Terry Lynn. *Answers from the Angels*. Tiburon, CA: H.J. Kramer Inc., 1993.

_____. *Creating with the Angels*. Tiburon, CA: H.J. Kramer Inc., 1993.

_____. *Guardians of Hope*. Tiburon, CA: H.J. Kramer Inc., 1992.

Messengers of Light. Tiburon, CA: H. J. Kramer Inc., 1990.

3. Theology Books that Include Angelology

Bancroft, Emery H. *Christian Theology*. Grand Rapids: Zondervan Publishing House, 1976.

Basic Christian Doctrines. Ed. Carl F.H. Henry. Grand Rapids: Baker Book House, 1983.

Berkhof, Louis. *Manual of Christian Doctrine*. Grand Rapids: Eerdmans Publishing Co., 1983.

_____. *Systematic Theology*. Grand Rapids: Eerdmans Publishing Co., 1982.

Boice, James Montgomery. *Foundations of the Christian Faith*. Downers Grove, IL: InterVarsity Press, 1981.

Buswell, James Oliver. *A Systematic Theology of the Christian Religion*. Grand Rapids: Zondervan Publishing House, 1979.

Calvin, John. *Institutes of the Christian Religion*, 8 vols. Ed. John T. McNeill. Trans. Ford Lewis Battles. Philadelphia: The Westminster Press, 1960.

Chafer, Lewis Sperry. *Systematic Theology*, 2 vols. Wheaton: Victor Books, 1988.

Chafer, Lewis Sperry; and Walvoord, John F. *Major Bible Themes*. Grand Rapids: Zondervan Publishing House, 1975.

Enns, Paul. *The Moody Handbook of Theology*. Chicago: Moody Press, 1989.

Erickson, Millard J. *Christian Theology*. Grand Rapids: Baker Book House, 1987.

Evans, William; and Coder, S. Maxwell. *The Great Doctrines of the Bible*. Chicago: Moody Press, 1974.

Hodge, Charles. *Systematic Theology*. Ed. Edward N. Gross. Grand Rapids: Baker Book House, 1988.

Hodges, A.A. *Outlines of Theology*. Grand Rapids: Zondervan Publishing House, 1972.

Lightner, Robert P. *Evangelical Theology*. Grand Rapids: Baker Book House, 1986.

Ryrie, Charles C. *Basic Theology*. Wheaton, IL: Victor Books, 1986.

_____. *A Survey of Bible Doctrine*. Chicago: Moody Press, 1980.

Strong, Augustus Hopkins. *Systematic Theology*. Old Tappan, NJ: Fleming H. Revell Company, 1979.

Thiessen, Henry Clarence. *Lectures in Systematic Theology*. Grand Rapids: Eerdmans Publishing Co., 1981.

4. Commentaries

Barclay, William. *The Gospel of John*. Philadelphia: Westminster Press, 1956.

Barnes, Albert. *Barnes' Notes on the Old and New Testaments*, 2 vols. Grand Rapids: Baker Book House, 1977.

Beckwith, Isbon T. *The Apocalypse of John*. Grand Rapids: Baker Book House, 1967.

Bruce, F.F. *The Book of Acts*. Grand Rapids: Eerdmans Publishing Co., 1986.

_____. *The Epistle to the Hebrews*. Grand Rapids: Eerdmans Publishing Co., 1979.

_____. *The Gospel of John*. Grand Rapids: Eerdmans Publishing Co., 1984.

Cole, R. Alan. *Exodus: An Introduction and Commentary*. Downers Grove, IL: InterVarsity Press, 1973.

Eadie, John. *A Commentary on the Greek Text of the Epistle of Paul to the Colossians*. Grand Rapids: Baker Book House, 1979.

English, E. Schuyler. *Studies in the Epistle to the Hebrews*. Neptune, NJ: Loizeaux Brothers, 1976.

Gaebelein, Arno C. *The Gospel of Matthew*. Neptune, NJ: Loizeaux Brothers, 1977.

Hendriksen, William. *Exposition of the Gospel According to John*. Grand Rapids: Baker Book House, 1976.

Henry, Matthew. *Commentary on the Whole Bible*. Grand Rapids: Zondervan Publishing House, 1974.

Jamieson, Robert; Fausset, A.R.; and Brown, David. *A Commentary—Critical, Experimental, and Practical—on the Old and New Testaments*. Grand Rapids: Eerdmans Publishing Co., 1973.

Keener, Craig S. *The IVP Bible Background Commentary: New Testament*. Downers Grove, IL: InterVarsity Press, 1993.

Keil C.F., and Delitzsch, Franz. *Biblical Commentary on the Old Testament*, 9 vols. Grand Rapids: Eerdmans Publishing Co., 1954.

Keller, Phillip. *A Shepherd Looks at Psalm 23*. Grand Rapids: Zondervan Publishing House, 1976.

Kidner, Derek. *Genesis: An Introduction and Commentary*. Downers Grove, IL: InterVarsity Press, 1967.

Lenski, R.C.H. *1 Corinthians*. Minneapolis, MN: Augsburg Publishing House, 1961.

_____. *First Peter*. Minneapolis, MN: Augsburg Publishing House, 1961.

_____. *Hebrews*. Minneapolis, MN: Augsburg Publishing House, 1961.

_____. *The Interpretation of St. John's Gospel*. Minneapolis, MN: Augsburg Publishing House, 1961.

Leupold, H.C. *Exposition of Genesis*. Grand Rapids: Baker Book House, 1980.

Lightfoot, J.B. *St. Paul's Epistles to the Colossians and to Philemon*. Grand Rapids: Zondervan Publishing House, 1979.

Lindsey, Hal. *There's a New World Coming*. Santa Ana, CA: Vision House Publishers, 1973.

MacArthur, John. *Hebrews*. Chicago: Moody Press, 1983.

_____. *The Superiority of Christ*. Chicago: Moody Press, 1986.

Morris, Leon. *The First Epistle of Paul to the Corinthians*, Tyndale New Testament Commentaries. Grand Rapids: Eerdmans Publishing Co., 1976.

_____. *The Gospel According to John*. Grand Rapids: Eerdmans Publishing Co., 1971.

_____. *The Gospel According to St. Luke*. Grand Rapids: Eerdmans Publishing Co., 1983.

Moule, H.C.G. *Studies in Colossians & Philemon*. Grand Rapids: Kregel Publications, 1977.

Newell, William R. *Hebrews: Verse by Verse*. Chicago: Moody Press, 1947.

Pink, Arthur W. *Exposition of the Gospel of John*. Swengel, PA: Bible Truth Depot, 1945.

Robertson, A.T. *Word Pictures*, 7 vols. Nashville: Broadman Press, 1930.

Robinson, Haddon W. *Psalm Twenty-Three*. Chicago: Moody Press, 1979.

Shedd, William G.T. *Romans*. New York: Scribner, 1879.

Stedman, Ray C. *Hebrews*. Downers Grove, IL: InterVarsity Press, 1992.

The Bible Knowledge Commentary, 2 vols. Eds. John F. Walvoord and Roy B. Zuck. Wheaton, IL: Victor Books, 1985.

The Expositor's Bible Commentary. Ed. Frank E. Gaebelein. Grand Rapids: Zondervan Publishing House, 1978.

The International Bible Commentary. Ed. F.F. Bruce. Grand Rapids: Zondervan Publishing House, 1979.

The Wycliffe Bible Commentary. Eds. Charles F. Pfeiffer and Everett F. Harrison. Chicago: Moody Press, 1974.

Toussaint, Stanley D. *Behold the King: A Study of Matthew*. Portland, OR: Multnomah Press, 1980.

Vincent, Marvin R. *Word Studies in the New Testament*, 4 vols. Grand Rapids: Eerdmans Publishing Co., 1975.

Walvoord, John F. *Daniel: The Key to Prophetic Revelation*. Chicago: Moody Press, 1981.

_____. *The Revelation of Jesus Christ*. Chicago: Moody Press, 1980.

Westcott, Brooke Foss. *The Epistle to the Hebrews*. Grand Rapids: Eerdmans Publishing Co., 1974.

Wuest, Kenneth S. *Wuest's Word Studies*, 4 vols. Grand Rapids: Eerdmans Publishing Co., 1953.

5. Reference Works

Brown, Francis; Driver, S.R.; and Briggs, Charles A. *A Hebrew and English Lexicon of the Old Testament*. Oxford: Clarendon Press, 1980.

Dictionary of Biblical Theology. Ed. Zavier Leon-Dufour. New York: The Seabury Press, 1983.

Draper's Book of Quotations for the Christian World. Ed. Edythe Draper. Grand Rapids: Baker Book House, 1992.

Evangelical Dictionary of Theology. Ed. Walter A. Elwell. Grand Rapids: Baker Books House, 1984.

International Standard Bible Encyclopedia, 4 vols. Ed. Geoffrey W. Bromiley. Grand Rapids: Eerdmans Publishing Co., 1986.

The New Bible Dictionary. Ed. J.D. Douglas. Wheaton, IL: Tyndale House Publishers, 1982.

The New International Dictionary of New Testament Theology, 3 vols. Ed. Colin Brown. Grand Rapids: Zondervan Publishing House, 1979.

The Zondervan Pictorial Encyclopedia of the Bible, 5 vols. Ed. Merrill C. Tenney. Grand Rapids: Zondervan Publishing House, 1978.

Theological Dictionary of the New Testament. Ed. Gerhard Kittle and Gerhard Friedrich. Abridged by Geoffrey W. Bromiley. Grand Rapids: Eerdmans Publishing Co., 1990.

Topical Analysis of the Bible. Ed. Walter A. Elwell. Grand Rapids: Baker Book House, 1991.

Vine's Expository Dictionary of Biblical Words. Ed. W.E. Vine, Merrill F. Unger, and William White, Jr. Nashville, TN: Thomas Nelson Publishers, 1985.

Zodhiates, Spiros. *The Complete Word Study Dictionary.* Chattanooga, TN: AMG Publishers, 1992.

6. Books on the Person and Work of Jesus Christ

Erickson, Millard J. *The Word Became Flesh: A Contemporary Incarnational Christology.* Grand Rapids: Baker Book House, 1991.

Geisler, Norman. *To Understand the Bible Look for Jesus.* Grand Rapids: Baker Book House, 1979.

McDowell, Josh; and Larson, Bart. *Jesus: A Biblical Defense of His Deity.* San Bernardino, CA: Here's Life Publishers, 1983.

Pentecost, J. Dwight. *The Words and Works of Jesus Christ.* Grand Rapids: Zondervan Publishing House, 1982.

Rhodes, Ron. *Christ Before the Manger: The Life and Times of the Preincarnate Christ.* Grand Rapids: Baker Book House, 1992.

Walvoord, John. *Jesus Christ Our Lord*. Chicago: Moody Press, 1980.

Warfield, Benjamin B. *The Lord of Glory*. Grand Rapids: Baker Book House, 1974.

_____. *The Person and Work of Christ*. Philadelphia: Presbyterian and Reformed Publishing, 1950.

7. Books on the Person and Work of Satan

Arnold, Clinton E. *Powers of Darkness: Principalities and Powers in Paul's Letters*. Downers Grove, IL: InterVarsity Press, 1992.

Chafer, Lewis Sperry. *Satan: His Motive and Methods*. Grand Rapids: Zondervan Publishing House, 1977.

Ice, Thomas; and Dean, Robert. *Overrun by Demons*. Eugene, OR: Harvest House Publishers, 1990.

Pentecost, J. Dwight. *Your Adversary the Devil*. Grand Rapids: Zondervan Publishing House, 1979.

Stedman, Ray C. *Spiritual Warfare*. Waco: Word Books, 1976.

Unger, Merrill F. *Demons in the World Today*. Wheaton, IL: Tyndale House Publishers, 1972.

Notes

Introduction: From the Voice of Angels

1. Craig S. Keener, *The IVP Bible Background Commentary* (Downers Grove, IL: InterVarsity Press, 1993), p. 779.

Chapter 1: Angels in the World Today

1. John Milton, in *Draper's Book of Quotations for the Christian World*, ed. Edythe Draper (Grand Rapids: Baker Book House, 1992), p. 386.

2. Fictitious names have been used to respect the privacy of the individuals involved.

3. Billy Graham, *Angels: God's Secret Agents* (Garden City, NY: Doubleday & Co., 1975), p. 152.

4. Timothy Jones, "Rumors of Angels: Telling Fact from Fad," *Christianity Today*, 5 April 1993, p. 22.

5. Cited in Graham, *Angels: God's Secret Agents*, p. 3.

6. Cited in Joan Wester Anderson, *Where Angels Walk* (New York: Ballantine Books, 1992), pp. 159-60.

7. *See* Corrie ten Boom, *Marching Orders for the End Battle* (Fort Washington, PA: Christian Literature Crusade, 1969), pp. 89-90.

8. Dawn Raffel, "Angels All Around Us: More and More People Claim They've Seen or Felt These Heavenly Messengers," *Redbook*, December 1992, p. 82.

9. Ibid.

10. L.W. Northrup, *Encounters with Angels* (Wheaton, IL: Tyndale House Publishers, 1993), p. 38.

11. A.C. Gaebelein, *What the Bible Says about Angels* (Grand Rapids: Baker Book House, 1993), p. 99.

12. "Angel Lore: Real-Life Encounters with Angels," *Ladies Home Journal*, December 1993, p. 192.

13. Ray C. Stedman, *Hebrews* (Downers Grove, IL: InterVarsity Press, 1992), p. 31.

Chapter 2: Flying High: Angel Popularity on the Rise

1. Craig Wilson, "Hark and Hallelujah! The Angels Are Here," *San Jose Mercury News*, 28 October 1992, p. 10D.

2. Cecelia Goodnow, "An Angel on Your Shoulder: More Mortals Are Getting a Boost from the Beyond," *San Francisco Examiner*, 25 August 1993, p. C7.

3. Alma Daniel, Timothy Wyllie, and Andrew Ramer, *Ask Your Angels* (New York: Ballantine Books, 1992), pp. 51-52.

4. Carl Herko, "Angels: Flying High from Newsletters to Pop Music—It's a Trend for Our Times," *Buffalo News*, 8 January 1993, p. G18.

5. Nancy Gibbs, "Angels Among Us," *Time*, 29 December 1993, electronic on-line version.

6. Kenneth L. Woodward, "Angels: Hark! America's Latest Search for Spiritual Meaning Has a Halo Effect," *Newsweek*, 27 December 1993, pp. 52-53.

7. Ibid.

8. Dawn Raffel, "Angels All Around Us: More and More People Claim They've Seen or Felt These Heavenly Messengers," *Redbook*, December 1992, p. 82.

9. Ibid.

10. "Angel Poll: What Americans Believe," *Time*, 29 December 1993, electronic on-line version.

11. Timothy Jones, "Rumors of Angels: Telling Fact from Fad," *Christianity Today*, 5 April 1993, p. 19.

12. Richard Scheinin, "Look Earthward Angel: Winged Messengers of Bible and Lore Fill a Spiritual Need in a Cold, Technical Age," *San Jose Mercury News*, 5 June 1993, p. 1C.

13. Goodnow, "An Angel on Your Shoulder," p. C7.

14. Woodward, "Angels: Hark!" pp. 54-55.

15. Ibid.

16. Herko, "Angels," p. G18.

17. Associated Press, "An Age for Angels: Spiritual, Commercial Interest in Heavenly Beings on the Rise," *Los Angeles Times*, 19 September 1992, p. 4.

18. Woodward, "Angels: Hark!" p. 54.

19. Gibbs, "Angels Among Us."

20. Ibid.

21. Ibid.

22. Jones, "Rumors of Angels," p. 20.

23. Goodnow, "An Angel on Your Shoulder," p. C7.

24. Susan Hall-Balduf, "Angel Aware: Graceful Stories from Heavens Afar," *Detroit Free Press*, 15 December 1993, p. 3E.

25. Eileen Elias Freeman, *Touched by Angels* (New York: Warner Books, 1993), p. 146.

26. Woodward, "Angels: Hark!" pp. 54-55.

27. Ibid.

28. Scheinin, "Look Earthward Angel," p. 1C.

29. Woodward, "Angels: Hark!" p. 57.

30. Ibid.

31. Freeman, *Touched by Angels*, p. xiii.

32. Scheinin, "Look Earthward Angel," p. 1C.

33. Tanya Barrientos, "Angel at Your Side?" *Orange County Register*, 24 December 1993, p. 1.

34. Robert C. Smith, *In the Presence of Angels: Stories from New Research on Angelic Influences* (Virginia Beach, VA: A.R.E. Press, 1993), p. x.

35. Associated Press, "An Age for Angels," p. 4.

36. Lisa Daniels, "Faithful Are Aflutter about Angels," *San Jose Mercury News*, 26 November 1992, p. 18H.

37. Associated Press, "An Age for Angels," p. 4.

38. Daniels, "Faithful Are Aflutter," p. 18H.

39. Veronique de Turenne, "Taking Wing: Protection and Comfort an Angel's Breath Away," *Orange County Register*, 27 December 1992, p. H1.

40. Ibid., p. H4.

41. Debora Vrana, "Family Copes with Grief by Believing in Angels," *Los Angeles Times*, 13 December 1993, p. 4.

42. Margaret Carlin, "Heavenly Ideas: Faith in Angels Sparks Boutiques, Networks," *Rocky Mountain News*, 22 December 1992, p. 49.

43. Woodward, "Angels: Hark!" p. 54.

44. Goodnow, "An Angel on Your Shoulder," p. C7.

45. Associated Press, "An Age for Angels," p. 4.

46. Terry Lynn Taylor, *Answers from the Angels: A Book of Angel Letters* (Tiburon, CA: H.J. Kramer Inc., 1993), p. 89, emphasis added.

47. Terry Lynn Taylor, *Messengers of Light: The Angels' Guide to Spiritual Growth* (Tiburon, CA: H.J. Kramer Inc., 1990), p. 19.

48. Ibid., p. xx.

49. Ibid., p. xvi.

50. Woodward, "Angels: Hark!" p. 57.

51. Ibid.

52. Ibid.

Chapter 3: Celestial Quackery

1. John Ronner, *Do You Have a Guardian Angel?* (Murfreesboro, TN: Mamre Press, 1993), p. 106.

2. Kenneth L. Woodward, "Angels: Hark! America's Latest Search for Spiritual Meaning Has a Halo Effect," *Newsweek*, 27 December 1993, p. 55, emphasis added.

3. Terry Lynn Taylor, *Messengers of Light: The Angels' Guide to Spiritual Growth* (Tiburon, CA: H.J. Kramer Inc., 1990), p. 9.

4. Ibid., p. xx.

5. Alma Daniel, Timothy Wyllie, and Andrew Ramer, *Ask Your Angels* (New York: Ballantine Books, 1992), pp. 3, 110, 124-25, 157.

6. Jane M. Howard, *Commune with the Angels* (Virginia Beach, VA: A.R.E. Press, 1992), p. 28.

7. In this chapter, many of the ideas about angels are rooted in the New Age movement. For a biblical response to channeling, visualization, the use of crystals, and other New Age concepts, see my book *The New Age Movement* (Grand Rapids: Zondervan Publishing House, 1994).

8. Daniel, Wyllie, and Ramer, *Ask Your Angels*, p. 173.

9. Timothy Jones, "Rumors of Angels: Telling Fact from Fad," *Christianity Today*, 5 April 1993, p. 19.

10. Ibid.

11. Alice Johnson, "Contacting Your Guardian Angel," *Longmont Daily Times* (Colorado), 2-3 May 1981, p. 3.

12. Ibid.

13. Ibid.

14. Ibid.

15. Terry Lynn Taylor, *Answers from the Angels: A Book of Angel Letters* (Tiburon, CA: H.J. Kramer Inc., 1993), p. 39.

16. Taylor, *Messengers of Light*, pp. 110-11.

17. Howard, *Commune with the Angels*, p. 81.

18. Taylor, *Messengers of Light*, p. 108.

19. Robert C. Smith, *In the Presence of Angels: Stories from New Research on Angelic Influences* (Virginia Beach, VA: A.R.E. Press, 1993), p. 74.

20. Ibid., p. 75

21. Howard, *Commune with the Angels*, p. 50.

22. Woodward, "Angels: Hark!" p. 55.

23. Howard, *Commune with the Angels*, p. 58.

24. Ibid., p. 71.

25. Ibid.

26. Ibid.

27. Daniel, Wyllie, and Ramer, *Ask Your Angels*, p. 237.

28. Ibid.

29. Taylor, *Messengers of Light*, p. 71.

30. Daniel, Wyllie, and Ramer, *Ask Your Angels*, p. 239.

31. Terry Lynn Taylor, *Creating with the Angels: An Angel-Guided Journey into Creativity* (Tiburon, CA: H.J. Kramer Inc. 1993), p. 74.

32. Ibid.

33. Daniel, Wyllie, and Ramer, *Ask Your Angels*, pp. 239-40.

34. Ronner, *Do You Have a Guardian Angel?* p. 106.

35. Taylor, *Messengers of Light*, pp. 118-19.

36. Marilyn Achiron, "The Halo Effect: Sophy Burnham's Alleged Encounter with a Guardian Angel," *People Weekly*, 17 May 1993, p. 75.

37. Cecelia Goodnow, "An Angel on Your Shoulder: More Mortals Are Getting a Boost from the Beyond," *San Francisco Examiner*, 25 August 1993, p. C7.

38. Pythia Peay, "The Presence of Angels," *Common Boundary*, January/February 1991, p. 30.

39. Achiron, "The Halo Effect," p. 75.

40. Eileen Elias Freeman, *Touched by Angels* (New York: Warner Books, 1993), p. 71.

41. Achiron, "The Halo Effect," p. 75.

42. Ronner, *Do You Have a Guardian Angel?* p. 110.

43. Terry Lynn Taylor, *Guardians of Hope: The Angels' Guide to Personal Growth* (Tiburon, CA: H.J. Kramer Inc. 1992), p. 63.

44. Smith, *In the Presence of Angels*, p. xviii.

45. Taylor, *Messengers of Light*, p. 26.

46. Howard, *Commune with the Angels*, p. 11.

47. Joan Wester Anderson, *Where Angels Walk* (New York: Ballantine Books, 1992), p. 20.

48. Sophy Burnham, *A Book of Angels* (New York: Ballantine Books, 1990), p. 111.

49. Nancy Gibbs, "Angels Among Us," *Time*, 29 December 1993, electronic on-line version.

50. Burnham, *A Book of Angels*, p. 110, emphasis added.

51. Peay, "The Presence of Angels," p. 30.

52. Burnham, *A Book of Angels*, p. 38.

53. Taylor, *Guardians of Hope*, p. xviii.

54. Taylor, *Creating with the Angels*, p. 54.

55. Taylor, *Answers from the Angels*, p. 12.

56. Howard, *Commune with the Angels*, p. 9.

57. Burnham, *A Book of Angels*, p. 38.

58. Peay, "The Presence of Angels," p. 30.

59. Daniel, Wyllie, and Ramer, *Ask Your Angels*, p. 174.

60. Taylor, *Messengers of Light*, p. 11.

61. Ibid., pp. 6, 16, 18-19, 21, 22, 80, 148.

62. Ibid., p. 50.

63. Taylor, *Guardians of Hope*, p. 47.

64. Freeman, *Touched by Angels*, p. xiv.

65. Daniel, Wyllie, and Rämer, *Ask Your Angels*, p. 4.

66. Taylor, *Messengers of Light*, p. 99; cf. Howard, *Commune with the Angels*, pp. 81-82.

67. Ibid., p. 78.

68. Taylor, *Answers from the Angels*, p. 70.

69. Taylor, *Messengers of Light*, p. 34.

70. Sophy Burnham, *Angel Letters* (New York: Ballantine Books, 1991), p. ix.

71. Taylor, *Messengers of Light*, p. 30.

72. Taylor, *Answers from the Angels*, p. 145.

73. Daniel, Wyllie, and Ramer, *Ask Your Angels*, pp. 300-301.

74. Ibid.

75. Taylor, *Guardians of Hope*, p. 71.

76. Ibid., p. 74.

77. Ibid.

78. Freeman, *Touched by Angels*, p. 68.

79. Ibid., pp. 69-70.

80. Ibid.

81. Ibid.

82. Taylor, *Messengers of Light*, p. 31.

83. Ibid., p. 43.

84. Ibid., p. 27.

85. Ibid.

86. Taylor, *Creating with the Angels*, p. 37.

87. Taylor, *Guardians of Hope*. p. xix, emphasis in original.

88. Ibid., p. xxiii.

89. Taylor, *Messengers of Light*, p. 13.

90. John Calvin, *Institutes of the Christian Religion*, ed. John T. McNeill, trans. Ford Lewis Battles (Philadelphia: The Westminster Press, 1960), 1.14.4.

Chapter 4: The Origin of Angels

1. Charles C. Ryrie, *Basic Theology* (Wheaton, IL: Victor Books, 1986), p. 122.

2. Ibid.

3. David Connolly, *In Search of Angels: A Celestial Sourcebook for Beginning Your Journey* (New York: Perigee Books, 1993), p. 69.

4. John C. Whitcomb, *The Early Earth* (Grand Rapids: Baker Book House, 1983), pp. 24-25.

5. Louis Berkhof, *Systematic Theology* (Grand Rapids: Eerdmans Publishing Co., 1982), p. 146.

6. William H. Baker, "Our Chariots of Fire," *Moody Monthly*, January 1986, p. 35.

7. John Eadie, *A Commentary on the Greek Text of the Epistle of Paul to the Colossians* (Grand Rapids: Baker Book House, 1979), p. 51.

8. *See* Marvin R. Vincent, *Word Studies in the New Testament*, vol. 3 (Grand Rapids: Eerdmans Publishing Co.,, 1975), pp. 469-70; Kenneth S. Wuest, *Wuest's Word Studies*, vol. 1 (Grand Rapids: Eerdmans Publishing Co., 1973), p. 184.

9. *The International Bible Commentary*, ed. F.F. Bruce (Grand Rapids: Zondervan, 1986), p. 1454, emphasis in original.

10. Cited in Connolly, *In Search of Angels*, p. 69.

11. *See* Roy Zuck, *Job* (Chicago: Moody Press, 1978), pp. 15, 166; cf. *The International Bible Commentary*, p. 546; and *The Wycliffe Bible Commentary*, eds. Charles F. Pfeiffer and Everett F. Harrison (Chicago: Moody Press, 1974), p. 461.

12. James Montgomery Boice, *Foundations of the Christian Faith* (Downers Grove, IL: InterVarsity Press, 1981), p. 167.

13. C. Fred Dickason, *Angels, Elect and Evil* (Chicago: Moody Press, 1978), p. 26.

14. Charles Hodge, *Systematic Theology*, abridged edition, ed. Edward N. Gross (Grand Rapids: Baker Book House, 1988), p. 232.

15. Dickason, *Angels, Elect and Evil*, p. 26.

16. Ryrie, *Basic Theology*, p. 127.

17. Berkhof, *Systematic Theology*, p. 145, emphasis added.

18. Dickason, *Angels, Elect and Evil*, pp. 40-41.

19. Henry Clarence Thiessen, *Lectures in Systematic Theology* (Grand Rapids: Eerdmans Publishing Co., 1981), p. 134, emphasis added, insert added.

20. Lewis Sperry Chafer, *Systematic Theology*, abridged edition, ed. John F. Walvoord (Wheaton, IL: Victor Books, 1989), p. 284.

Chapter 5: The Nature of Angels

1. Cited by Lisa Daniels, "Faithful Are Aflutter about Angels," *San Jose Mercury News*, 26 November 1992, p. 18H.

2. "Angel Poll: What Americans Believe," *Time*, 29 December 1993, electronic on-line version.

3. G.W. Bromiley, "Angels," in *Evangelical Dictionary of Theology*, ed. Walter A. Elwell (Grand Rapids: Baker Book House, 1984), p. 46.

4. Cited in David Connolly, *In Search of Angels: A Celestial Sourcebook for Beginning Your Journey* (New York: Perigee Books, 1993), p. 17.

5. Henry Clarence Thiessen, *Lectures in Systematic Theology* (Grand Rapids: Eerdmans Publishing Co., 1981), p. 133.

6. C. Fred Dickason, *Angels, Elect and Evil* (Chicago: Moody Press, 1978), p. 56.

7. Louis Berkhof, *Manual of Christian Doctrine* (Grand Rapids: Eerdmans Publishing Co. 1983), p. 100.

8. Lewis Sperry Chafer and John F. Walvoord, *Major Bible Themes* (Grand Rapids: Zondervan Publishing House, 1975), p. 152.

9. Charles C. Ryrie, *Basic Theology* (Wheaton, IL: Victor Books, 1986), p. 126.

10. Augustus Hopkins Strong, *Systematic Theology: A Compendium* (Old Tappan, NJ: Fleming H. Revell Company, 1979), p. 445.

11. William H. Baker, "Our Chariots of Fire," *Moody Monthly*, January 1986, p. 35.

12. Billy Graham, *Angels: God's Secret Agents* (Garden City, NY: Doubleday & Co., 1975), p. 24.

13. Ibid., p. 28.

14. Dickason, *Angels, Elect and Evil*, p. 33.

15. Millard J. Erickson, *Christian Theology* (Grand Rapids: Baker Book House, 1987), p. 440.

16. Dickason, *Angels, Elect and Evil*, p. 39.

17. Graham, *Angels: God's Secret Agents*, p. 19.

18. Dickason, *Angels, Elect and Evil*, p. 35.

19. Ibid., p. 44.

20. Strong, *Systematic Theology*, p. 445.

21. Ryrie, *Basic Theology*, p. 125.

22. Dickason, *Angels, Elect and Evil*, p. 34.

23. Baker, "Our Chariots of Fire," p. 35.

24. Ryrie, *Basic Theology*, p. 126.

Chapter 6: The Organization of Angels

1. A. Duane Litfin, "Evangelical Feminism: Why Traditionalists Reject It," *Bibliotheca Sacra*, July-September 1979, p. 267.

2. David Connolly, *In Search of Angels: A Celestial Sourcebook for Beginning Your Journey* (New York: Perigee Books, 1993), p. 78.

3. Kenneth L. Woodward, "Angels: Hark! America's Latest Search for Spiritual Meaning Has a Halo Effect," *Newsweek*, 27 December 1993, p. 57.

4. Ibid., p. 57.

5. Connolly, *In Search of Angels*, p. 77.

6. C. Fred Dickason, *Angels, Elect and Evil* (Chicago: Moody Press, 1978), p. 86.

7. Charles C. Ryrie, *Basic Theology* (Wheaton, IL: Victor Books, 1986), p. 128.

8. Billy Graham, *Angels: God's Secret Agents* (Garden City, NY: Doubleday & Co., 1975), p. 40.

9. *See* J.B. Lightfoot, *Saint Paul's Epistles to the Colossians and to Philemon* (Grand Rapids: Zondervan Publishing House, 1959), p. 152.

10. Louis Berkhof, *Systematic Theology* (Grand Rapids: Eerdmans Publishing Co., 1982), p. 147. John McRay similarly says, "These are designations in early Jewish and Christian documents for heavenly powers who reside in the regions between God and man." *Evangelical Commentary on the Bible*, ed. Walter A. Elwell (Grand Rapids: Baker Book House, 1989), p. 1054.

11. John Calvin, *Institutes of the Christian Religion*, ed. John T. McNeill, trans. Ford Lewis Battles (Philadelphia: The Westminster Press, 1960), 1.14.5; cf. Lightfoot, *Saint Paul's Epistles to the Colossians and to Philemon*, p. 154.

12. T.K. Abbott, *The International Critical Commentary: The Epistles to the Ephesians and to the Colossians* (Edinburgh: T. & T. Clark, 1979), p. 216.

13. Ibid.

14. *See* Lightfoot, *Saint Paul's Epistles to the Colossians and to Philemon*, p. 154.

15. Henry Clarence Thiessen, *Lectures in Systematic Theology* (Grand Rapids: Eerdmans Publishing Co., 1981), p. 140.

16. Lewis Sperry Chafer, *Systematic Theology*, abridged edition, ed. John F. Walvoord (Wheaton, IL: Victor Books, 1989), p. 285.

17. Lightfoot, *Saint Paul's Epistles to the Colossians and to Philemon*, p. 153.

18. A.A. Hodges, *Outlines of Theology* (Grand Rapids: Zondervan Publishing House, 1972), p. 251.

19. Ryrie, *Basic Theology*, p. 128.

20. Dickason, *Angels, Elect and Evil*, p. 68, emphasis added.

21. *International Standard Bible Encyclopedia*, ed. Geoffrey W. Bromiley, vol. 3 (Grand Rapids: Eerdmans Publishing Co., 1986), p. 347.

22. Clinton E. Arnold, *Powers of Darkness: Principalities and Powers in Paul's Letters* (Downers Grove, IL: InterVarsity Press, 1992), p. 63.

23. Berkhof, *Systematic Theology*, p. 147.

24. James Montgomery Boice, *Foundations of the Christian Faith* (Downers Grove, IL: InterVarsity Press, 1981), p. 168.

25. Dickason, *Angels, Elect and Evil*, p. 67.

26. Ray Stedman, *Hebrews* (Downers Grove, IL: InterVarsity Press, 1992), p. 29.

27. Boice, *Foundations of the Christian Faith*, p. 168.

28. Charles Dyer, "Ezekiel," in *The Bible Knowledge Commentary*, Old Testament, eds. John F. Walvoord and Roy B. Zuck (Wheaton, IL: Victor Books, 1985), p. 1228.

29. Rene Pache, *The Future Life* (Chicago: Moody Press, 1962), p. 102.

30. Dickason, *Angels, Elect and Evil*, p. 63.

31. Ibid., p. 65.

32. Ibid., p. 66, emphasis in original.

33. Ibid., p. 65.

34. Hodges, *Outlines of Theology*, p. 250.

35. Dickason, *Angels, Elect and Evil*, p. 70.

36. *The New International Dictionary of New Testament Theology*, ed. Colin Brown, s.v. "Gabriel" (Grand Rapids: Zondervan Publishing House, 1979), p. 103.

37. Boice, *Foundations of the Christian Faith*, p. 168.

38. A.C. Gaebelein, *What the Bible Says about Angels* (Grand Rapids: Baker Book House, 1993), p. 17.

39. Litfin, "Evangelical Feminism: Why Traditionalists Reject It," p. 267.

Chapter 7: Titles of Angels

1. Henri Cazelles, "Name," in *Dictionary of Biblical Theology*, ed. Zavier Leon-Dufour (New York: The Seabury Press, 1983), p. 377.

2. Henry Clarence Thiessen, *Lectures in Systematic Theology* (Grand Rapids: Eerdmans Publishing Co., 1981), p. 139.

3. Emery H. Bancroft, *Christian Theology* (Grand Rapids: Zondervan Publishing House, 1976), p. 311.

4. James Oliver Buswell, *A Systematic Theology of the Christian Religion* (Grand Rapids: Zondervan Publishing House, 1979), 1:105.

5. Charles C. Ryrie, *Basic Theology* (Wheaton, IL: Victor Books, 1986), p. 248.

6. Benjamin B. Warfield, *The Person and Work of Christ* (Philadelphia: Presbyterian and Reformed Publishing, 1950), p. 77.

7. C.F. Keil and F. Delitzsch, *Commentary on the Old Testament*, vol. 6 (Grand Rapids: Eerdmans Publishing Co., 1986), pp. 273-78; cf. Robert Jamieson, A.R. Fausset, and David Brown, *A Commentary—Critical, Experimental, and Practical—on the Old and New Testaments* (Grand Rapids: Eerdmans Publishing Co., 1973), p. 508.

8. *See* R. Laird Harris, "Proverbs," in *The Wycliffe Bible Commentary*, eds. Charles F. Pfeiffer and Everett F. Harrison (Chicago: Moody Press, 1974), p. 581.

9. Albert Barnes, *Notes on the New Testament* (Grand Rapids: Baker Book House, 1977), p. 45.

10. Ray C. Stedman, *Hebrews* (Downers Grove, IL: InterVarsity Press, 1992), p. 31.

11. Ibid.

12. Barnes, *Notes on the New Testament*, p. 45.

13. Ibid., p. 46.

14. Ibid., p. 47.

15. C. Fred Dickason, *Angels, Elect and Evil* (Chicago: Moody Press, 1978), p. 59.

16. John Calvin, *Institutes of the Christian Religion*, ed. John T. McNeill, trans. Ford Lewis Battles (Philadelphia: The Westminster Press, 1960), 1.14.5.

17. Dickason, *Angels, Elect and Evil*, p. 59.

18. See *The International Bible Commentary*, ed. F.F. Bruce (Grand Rapids: Zondervan Publishing House, 1986), p. 281.

19. Thiessen, *Lectures in Systematic Theology*, p. 139.

20. John F. Walvoord, *Daniel: The Key to Prophetic Revelation* (Chicago: Moody Press, 1981), p. 102.

21. Ibid.

Chapter 8: The Angel of the Lord

1. John Calvin, *Institutes of the Christian Religion*, ed. John T. McNeill, trans. Ford Lewis Battles, vol. 1 (Philadelphia: The Westminster Press, 1960), p. 133, inserts added.

2. See R. Alan Cole, *Exodus: An Introduction and Commentary* (Downers Grove, IL: InterVarsity Press, 1973), p. 65.

3. Guy B. Funderburk notes, "[The Angel] was not restricted to executing a single order, but, like Jesus, He spoke with authority as though He were God Himself. Only the Logos, or some other manifest personification of God, would be able to do that." ("Angel," in *The Zondervan Pictorial Encyclopedia of the Bible*, ed. Merrill C. Tenney, vol. 1 [Grand Rapids: Zondervan Publishing House, 1978], p. 163.)

4. See H.C. Leupold, *Exposition of Genesis*, vol. 1 (Grand Rapids: Baker Book House, 1980), p. 503.

5. Ron Rhodes, *Christ Before the Manger: The Life and Times of the Preincarnate Christ* (Grand Rapids: Baker Book House, 1992).

6. See C.F. Keil and Franz Delitzsch, "Zechariah," *Biblical Commentary on the Old Testament* (Grand Rapids: Eerdmans Publishing Co., 1954), p. 235.

7. See Rhodes, *Christ Before the Manger*, p. 84.

8. John Walvoord notes, "As the Angel of Jehovah characteristically appears in bodily, usually human form, He could not be the Holy Spirit who does not appear bodily, except in the rare instance of appearing in the form of a

dove at the baptism of Christ" (*Jesus Christ Our Lord* [Chicago: Moody Press, 1980], p. 46).

9. Ibid., p. 54.

10. Rhodes, *Christ Before the Manger*, p. 86.

11. Ibid., p. 87.

12. Ibid.

13. Norman Geisler, *To Understand the Bible Look for Jesus* (Grand Rapids: Baker Book House, 1979), p. 67.

14. *See* Josh McDowell and Bart Larson, *Jesus: A Biblical Defense of His Deity* (San Bernardino, CA: Here's Life Publishers, Inc., 1983), p. 79.

15. Irenaeus, *Against Heresies* (4.10.1); cited in Walvoord, *Jesus Christ Our Lord*, p. 55.

16. *First Apology*, lxii; lxiii; compare with Martyr's *Dialogue with Trypho*, p. 59; *See* McDowell and Larson, *Jesus: A Biblical Defense of His Deity*, p. 79.

17. Tertullian, *Against Praxeas*, p. 16; *see also* Tertullian's *Against Marcion*, 2.27; cited in Walvoord, *Jesus Christ Our Lord*, p. 55.

18. *See* Richard Watson, *Theological Institutes*, 2 vols., 29th ed. (New York: Nelson & Philipps, 1850), 1:501-2; quoted in Walvoord, *Jesus Christ Our Lord*, p. 55.

19. Charles Hodge, *Systematic Theology*, abridged edition, ed. Edward N. Gross (Grand Rapids: Baker Book House, 1988), p. 177.

20. Francis Brown, S.R. Driver, and Charles A. Briggs, *A Hebrew and English Lexicon of the Old Testament* (Oxford: Clarendon Press, 1980), p. 521. *See also* H. Bietenhard, s.v. "Angel," in *New Testament Theology*, ed. Colin Brown, vol. 1 (Grand Rapids: Zondervan Publishing House, 1979), pp. 101-103.

21. Calvin, *Institutes of the Christian Religion*, p. 133, emphasis in original.

Chapter 9: Celestial Spectators of Planet Earth

1. Rene Pache, *The Future Life* (Chicago: Moody Press, 1980), p. 116.

2. *See* Louis A. Barbieri, *First and Second Peter* (Chicago: Moody Press, 1979), p. 40.

3. *See The Bible Knowledge Commentary*, eds. John F. Walvoord and Roy B. Zuck (Wheaton, IL: Victor Books, 1985), p. 30.

4. A.C. Gaebelein, *What the Bible Says about Angels* (Grand Rapids: Baker Book House, 1993), p. 55.

5. For a full list of the prophecies that deal with the coming of the future Redeemer, see the Appendix in my book *Christ Before the Manger: The Life and Times of the Preincarnate Christ* (Grand Rapids: Baker Book House, 1992).

6. Gaebelein, *What the Bible Says about Angels*, p. 65.

7. Leon Morris, *The Gospel According to John* (Grand Rapids: Eerdmans Publishing Co., 1987), p. 815.

8. Gaebelein, *What the Bible Says about Angels*, p. 81.

9. Ibid., p. 67.

Chapter 10: Servants of the Most High

1. Millard J. Erickson, *Christian Theology* (Grand Rapids: Baker Book House, 1987), p. 441.

2. Nancy Gibbs, "Angels Among Us," *Time*, 29 December 1993, electronic on-line version.

3. Cecelia Goodnow, "An Angel on Your Shoulder: More Mortals Are Getting a Boost from the Beyond," *San Francisco Examiner*, 25 August 1993, p. C7.

4. Kenneth L. Woodward, "Angels: Hark! America's Latest Search for Spiritual Meaning Has a Halo Effect," *Newsweek*, 27 December 1993, pp. 54-55.

5. *See Theological Dictionary of the New Testament*, ed. Geoffrey W. Bromiley (Grand Rapids: Eerdmans Publishing Co., 1990), p. 14.

6. John Calvin, *Institutes of the Christian Religion*, ed. John T. McNeill, trans. Ford Lewis Battles (Philadelphia: The Westminster Press, 1960), 1.14.11.

7. Charles C. Ryrie, *Basic Theology* (Wheaton, IL: Victor Books, 1986), p. 133.

8. C. Fred Dickason, *Angels, Elect and Evil* (Chicago: Moody Press, 1978), p. 12.

9. Bernard Ramm, "Angels," in *Basic Christian Doctrines*, ed. Carl F.H. Henry (Grand Rapids: Baker Book House, 1983), p. 66.

10. Erickson, *Christian Theology*, p. 441.

11. G.W. Bromiley, "Angels," in *Evangelical Dictionary of Theology*, ed. Walter A. Elwell (Grand Rapids: Baker Books House, 1984), p. 46.

12. Timothy Jones, "Rumors of Angels: Telling Fact from Fad," *Christianity Today*, 5 April 1993, p. 21.

13. Calvin, *Institutes of the Christian Religion*, 1.14.12.

14. Ibid.

15. *See* Louis Berkhof, *Systematic Theology* (Grand Rapids: Eerdmans Publishing Co., 1982), p. 147.

Chapter 11: Ministers to Jesus Christ

1. Rene Pache, *The Future Life* (Chicago: Moody Press, 1962), p. 106.

2. Albert Barnes, *Barnes's Notes on the Old & New Testaments* (Grand Rapids: Baker Book House, 1976), p. 248.

3. Laurence E. Porter, "Luke," in *The International Bible Commentary*, ed. F.F. Bruce (Grand Rapids: Zondervan Publishing House, 1986), p. 1188.

4. John A. Martin, "Luke," in *The Bible Knowledge Commentary*, eds. John F. Walvoord and Roy B. Zuck (Wheaton, IL: Victor Books, 1983), p. 205.

5. J. Dwight Pentecost, *The Words and Works of Jesus Christ* (Grand Rapids: Zondervan Publishing House, 1982), p. 45.

6. Though the text says that "an angel of the Lord" appeared to Joseph, this is not the same as *the* Angel of the Lord, who was a preincarnate appearance of Christ in Old Testament times. See my book *Christ Before the Manger: The Life and Times of the Preincarnate Christ* (Grand Rapids: Baker Book House, 1992).

7. Millard J. Erickson, *The Word Became Flesh: A Contemporary Incarnational Christology* (Grand Rapids: Baker Book House, 1991), p. 24.

8. Pentecost, *The Words and Works of Jesus Christ*, p. 55.

9. Benjamin B. Warfield, *The Lord of Glory* (Grand Rapids: Baker Book House, 1974), p. 108.

10. Leon Morris, *The Gospel According to St. Luke* (Grand Rapids: Eerdmans Publishing Co., 1983), p. 86.

11. Spiros Zodhiates, *The Complete Word Study Dictionary* (Chattanooga, TN: AMG Publishers, 1992), p. 429.

12. Ibid., p. 591.

13. Billy Graham, *Angels: God's Secret Agents* (Garden City, NY: Doubleday & Co., 1975), p. 128.

Chapter 12: Angels Among *Us*

1. Billy Graham, *Angels: God's Secret Agents* (Garden City, NY: Doubleday & Co., 1975), p. 25.

2. G.W. Bromiley, "Angels," in *Evangelical Dictionary of Theology*, ed. Walter A. Elwell (Grand Rapids: Baker Books House, 1984), p. 47.

3. Cited in David Connolly, *In Search of Angels: A Celestial Sourcebook for Beginning Your Journey* (New York: Perigee Books, 1993), p. 48.

4. Graham, *Angels: God's Secret Agents*, p. 92.

5. Ibid., p. 95.

6. Ibid., p. 15.

7. Ibid., p. 74.

8. *See* William H. Baker, "Our Chariots of Fire," *Moody Monthly*, January 1986, p. 36.

9. Rene Pache, *The Future Life* (Chicago: Moody Press, 1962), p. 111.

10. Millard J. Erickson, *Christian Theology* (Grand Rapids: Baker Book House, 1987), p. 435.

11. Connolly, *In Search of Angels*, p. 36.

12. Louis Berkhof, *Systematic Theology* (Grand Rapids: Eerdmans Publishing Co., 1982), pp. 147-48; cf. Timothy Jones, "Rumors of Angels: Telling Fact from Fad," *Christianity Today*, 5 April 1993, p. 21.

13. Erickson, *Christian Theology*, p. 445.

14. John Calvin, *Institutes of the Christian Religion*, ed. John T. McNeill, trans. Ford Lewis Battles (Philadelphia: The Westminster Press, 1960), 1.14.7.

15. Ibid.

16. Ibid., 1.14.11.

17. Ibid., 1.14.6.

18. Ibid., 1.14.8.

19. James Montgomery Boice, *Foundations of the Christian Faith* (Downers Grove, IL: InterVarsity Press, 1981), p. 170.

20. Graham, *Angels: God's Secret Agents*, p. 154.

21. Ibid., p. 148.

22. Ibid., p. 152.

23. Ibid., p. 155.

24. Cecelia Goodnow, "An Angel on Your Shoulder: More Mortals Are Getting a Boost from the Beyond," *San Francisco Examiner*, 25 August 1993, p. C7.

25. Pythia Peay, "The Presence of Angels," *Common Boundary*, January/February 1991, p. 30.

26. Marilyn Achiron, "The Halo Effect: Sophy Burnham's Alleged Encounter with a Guardian Angel," *People Weekly*, 17 May 1993, p. 75.

27. Sophy Burnham, *A Book of Angels* (New York: Ballantine Books, 1990), p. 110, emphasis added.

28. C. Fred Dickason, *Angels, Elect and Evil* (Chicago: Moody Press, 1978), p. 37.

29. Charles Hodge, *Systematic Theology*, abridged edition, ed. Edward N. Gross (Grand Rapids: Baker Book House, 1988), p. 234.

30. Graham, *Angels: God's Secret Agents*, p. 25.

Chapter 13: Angels Among *Them*

1. Susan Hall-Balduf, "Angel Aware: Graceful Stories from Heavens Afar," *Detroit Free Press*, 15 December 1993, p. 3E.

2. Pythia Peay, "The Presence of Angels," *Common Boundary*, January/February 1991, p. 30.

3. Sophy Burnham, *A Book of Angels* (New York: Ballantine Books, 1990), p. 38.

4. Ibid.

5. Alma Daniel, Timothy Wyllie, and Andrew Ramer, *Ask Your Angels* (New York: Ballantine Books, 1992), p. 174.

6. *See* William Evans and S. Maxwell Coder, *The Great Doctrines of the Bible* (Chicago: Moody Press, 1974), p. 219.

7. *See* C. Fred Dickason, *Angels, Elect and Evil* (Chicago: Moody Press, 1978), p. 98.

8. Ibid., p. 44.

9. Cited in Billy Graham, *Angels: God's Secret Agents* (Garden City, NY: Doubleday & Co., 1975), p. 3.

10. Peay, "The Presence of Angels," p. 30.

Chapter 14: Fallen Angels

1. Erwin W. Lutzer; cited in *Draper's Book of Quotations for the Christian World*, ed. Edythe Draper (Grand Rapids: Baker Book House, 1992), p. 543.

2. This view is held by numerous scholars, including Paul Enns, *The Moody Handbook of Theology* (Chicago: Moody Press, 1989), p. 292; Merrill F. Unger, *Demons in the World Today* (Wheaton, IL: Tyndale House Publishers, 1972), p. 8; Thomas Ice and Robert Dean, *Overrun by Demons* (Eugene, OR: Harvest House Publishers, 1990), pp. 37-57; Lewis Sperry Chafer, *Satan: His Motive and Methods* (Grand Rapids: Zondervan Publishing House, 1977), p. 15; J. Dwight Pentecost, *Your Adversary the Devil* (Grand Rapids: Zondervan Publishing House, 1979), chapter 1; and C. Fred Dickason, *Angels, Elect and Evil* (Chicago: Moody Press, 1978), p. 118.

3. *See The Bible Knowledge Commentary*, eds. John F. Walvoord and Roy B. Zuck (Wheaton, IL: Victor Books, 1985), p. 1283.

4. Charles C. Ryrie, *Basic Theology* (Wheaton, IL: Victor Books, 1986), p. 142; cf. Pentecost, *Your Adversary the Devil*, p. 11.

5. Ice and Dean, *Overrun by Demons*, p. 40.

6. Ibid.

7. *The Bible Knowledge Commentary*, p. 1283.

8. Donald Grey Barnhouse, *The Invisible War* (Grand Rapids: Zondervan Publishing House, 1965), pp. 26-27.

9. *The Bible Knowledge Commentary*, p. 1061.

10. Dickason, *Angels, Elect and Evil*, p. 130.

11. Ibid., p. 133.

12. Ryrie, *Basic Theology*, p. 145.

13. *See* Dickason, *Angels, Elect and Evil*, p. 134.

14. Ryrie, *Basic Theology*, p. 145.

15. Ice and Dean, *Overrun by Demons*, p. 46.

16. Dickason, *Angels, Elect and Evil*, p. 122.

17. Charles Hodge, *Systematic Theology*, ed. Edward N. Gross (Grand Rapids: Baker Book House, 1988), p. 235.

18. Ray C. Stedman, *Spiritual Warfare* (Waco: Word Books, 1976), p. 22.

19. Henry C. Thiessen, *Lectures in Systematic Theology* (Grand Rapids: Eerdmans Publishing Co., 1981), p. 142.

20. Lewis Sperry Chafer; cited in Ice and Dean, *Overrun by Demons*, p. 60.

21. Thiessen, *Lectures in Systematic Theology*, p. 142.

22. Charles C. Ryrie, *Balancing the Christian Life* (Chicago: Moody Press, 1978), p. 124.

23. Charles C. Ryrie, *A Survey of Bible Doctrine* (Chicago: Moody Press, 1980), p. 94.

24. Ryrie, *Basic Theology*, p. 147.

25. Ryrie, *Balancing the Christian Life*, p. 124.

26. *See* Clinton E. Arnold, *Powers of Darkness: Principalities and Powers in Paul's Letters* (Downers Grove, IL: InterVarsity Press, 1992), chapter 7.

27. Enns, *The Moody Handbook of Theology*, p. 294.

28. This is the view of Enns, *The Moody Handbook of Theology*, p. 294.

29. See Ryrie, *Basic Theology*, p. 159.

30. Merrill F. Unger; cited in Thiessen, *Lectures in Systematic Theology*, p. 141.

31. Unger, *Demons in the World Today*, p. 28.

32. Millard J. Erickson, *Christian Theology* (Grand Rapids: Baker Book House, 1987), p. 450.

33. Ryrie, *Basic Theology*, p. 159, insert added; cf. Unger, *Demons in the World Today*, pp. 15-16.

34. *See* Ryrie, *Basic Theology*, p. 159; cf. Arnold, *Powers of Darkness*, pp. 65-67.

35. *See* Charles C. Ryrie, *You Mean the Bible Teaches That...* (Chicago: Moody Press, 1976), p. 99.

36. *See* Enns, *The Moody Handbook of Theology*, p. 297.

37. Charles C. Ryrie, cited in Enns, *The Moody Handbook of Theology*, p. 298.

38. *See* Erickson, *Christian Theology*, p. 449.

39. Enns, *The Moody Handbook of Theology*, p. 298.

40. *See* Ice and Dean, *Overrun by Demons*, pp. 119-20.

41. *See* Ice and Dean, *Overrun by Demons*, chapter 8; and Berit Kjos, *A Wardrobe from the King: 8 Studies on the Armor of God* (Wheaton, IL: Victor Books, 1992).

42. Stedman, *Spiritual Warfare*, p. 114.

43. Erickson, *Christian Theology*, p. 449.

Chapter 15: Anticipating Eternity

1. John Baillie; cited in *Draper's Book of Quotations for the Christian World*, ed. Edythe Draper (Grand Rapids: Baker Book House, 1992), p. 180.

2. Erich Sauer, *From Eternity to Eternity* (Grand Rapids: Eerdmans Publishing Co., 1979), p. 30.

3. Hope MacDonald, *When Angels Appear* (Grand Rapids: Zondervan Publishing House, 1982), p. 27, emphasis in original.

Also by Ron Rhodes

Reasoning from the Scriptures with the Jehovah's Witnesses

Many outstanding features make this the *complete* hands-on guide to sharing the truth of God's Word in a loving, gracious way: Side-by-side comparisons of the *New World Translation* and the Bible; point-by-point lists of the favorite tactics and arguments used by the Witnesses; and hundreds of penetrating questions you can ask to challenge the Jehovah's Witnesses' confidence in the Watchtower Society. If you have room for only one book about Jehovah's Witnesses in your library, you'll want to make sure it is this one!

The Culting of America

This highly charged and meticulously researched book goes beyond exposing the growing darkness to shattering that darkness with the truth of the gospel. *The Culting of America* gets to the quick of the matter in brisk chapters that show how cults are achieving mainstream status in our society. This book shows how Christians can make a difference in school, in the workplace, in the church, and in society.

Other Good Harvest House Reading

THE NEW SPIRITUALITY
by *Dave Hunt* and *T.A. McMahon*

Many respected experts predict that America is at the threshold of a glorious New Age. Other equally notable observers warn that Eastern mysticism, at the heart of the New Age movement, will eventually corrupt Western civilization. *Who is right?* Will we be able to distinguish between the true hope of the Gospel and the false hope of the New Age?

Dave Hunt and T.A. McMahon break down the most brilliant arguments of the most-respected New Age leaders and present overwhelming evidence for the superiority of the Christian faith.

CHRISTIANITY IN CRISIS
by *Hank Hanegraaff*

Christianity in Crisis confronts head-on a cancer that is ravaging the body of Christ. Influential teachers are utilizing the power of the airwaves as well as scores of books, tapes, and magazines to distort the biblical concept of the Creator and promote antibiblical doctrines that boggle the mind. The result is nothing less than a systematic subversion of the historic Christian faith. In addition to exposing darkness to light, *Christianity in Crisis* provides solutions for averting this crisis and restoring a Christianity centered in Christ.

OVERRUN BY DEMONS
by *Thomas Ice* and *Robert Dean*

Just as an interest in spirits is capturing the minds and imagination of the world today, so an emphasis on angels, demons, and spiritual warfare is capturing the attention of Christians. In a world caught in a web of spiritual intrigue and confusion, Christians must measure current fads in spiritual warfare against the standard of biblical truth. In *Overrun by Demons*, authors Thomas Ice and Robert Dean skillfully reveal the biblical strategy for winning in the spiritual warfare we are a part of every day.

Dear Reader:

We would appreciate hearing from you regarding this Harvest House nonfiction book. It will enable us to continue to give you the best in Christian publishing.

1. What most influenced you to purchase *Angels Among Us*?
   ☐ Author   ☐ Recommendations
   ☐ Subject matter   ☐ Cover/Title
   ☐ Backcover copy   ☐ _____

2. Where did you purchase this book?
   ☐ Christian bookstore   ☐ Grocery store
   ☐ General bookstore   ☐ Other
   ☐ Department store

3. Your overall rating of this book:
   ☐ Excellent ☐ Very good ☐ Good ☐ Fair ☐ Poor

4. How likely would you be to purchase other books by this author?
   ☐ Very likely   ☐ Not very likely
   ☐ Somewhat likely   ☐ Not at all

5. What types of books most interest you?
   (check all that apply)
   ☐ Women's Books   ☐ Fiction
   ☐ Marriage Books   ☐ Biographies
   ☐ Current Issues   ☐ Children's Books
   ☐ Christian Living   ☐ Youth Books
   ☐ Bible Studies   ☐ Other _____

6. Please check the box next to your age group.
   ☐ Under 18   ☐ 25-34   ☐ 45-54
   ☐ 18-24   ☐ 35-44   ☐ 55 and over

Mail to: Editorial Director
Harvest House Publishers
1075 Arrowsmith
Eugene, OR 97402

Name _____

Address _____

City _____ State _____ Zip _____

**Thank you for helping us to help you
in future publications!**